THINGS WE NEED TO KNOW

and no one is telling us

William Crumley C.S.C.

OPTION PRESS
April 2016

Dedication

I dedicate this book to

Brother Thomas Combs C.S.C.

Tom kept on me until I wrote it

Thanks Tom

INDEX

Introduction

Post war development of IG Farben

The Heritage of IG Farben

SAFEHAVEN

Operation Paperclip

BAYER

Is USA heading for New world order?

How we got ourselves into this mess

IS THERE ANY HOPE?

After Thought

INTRODUCTION

The world is constantly in transition like each of us. We are in transition, in need of rehabilitation. That transition, that rehabilitation can be good or bad. The final transition and rehabilitation is death. In death the words we speak can leave a different legacy than the words we spoke. For a good legacy to remain those who hear the words must act out of love and not fear. For example, there is the legacy of Jesus Christ: "Come, blessed by my Father, inherit the kingdom prepared for you from the foundation of the world. I was hungry and you gave me food. I was thirsty and you gave me drink, a stranger and you welcomed me, naked and you gave me clothing, ill and you cared for me, in prison and you visited me ... Whatever you did for a least brother of mine, you did for me."

We inherit the legacy of Jesus. We don't earn a legacy. It is the gift of love, a love more powerful than all hatred, a legacy which could change our life. That legacy of Jesus Christ was not enough to make change. In order to remain alive his hearers had to live out what he spoke. He lived 2000 years ago. Because his followers lived out his words, those words are not quotes that are dead and died with the one who said them. Those who lived out his legacy also died. For centuries people have lived out his legacy. Today they are kept alive by people willing to live by these words, to live out his legacy. One of those persons is Oscar Romero. He taught the following lessons as: legacy

"Peace is not the product of terror or fear. Peace is not the silence of cemeteries Peace is not the silent result of violent repression. ... Peace is generosity. It is right and it is duty. Peace is dynamism. I don't want to be an anti, against anybody. I simply want to be the builder of a great affirmation:, the affirmation of God, who loves us and wants to save us. By contrast, whoever out of love for God gives oneself to the service of others will live, like the grain of wheat that dies, but only apparently ... Only in undoing itself does it produce the harvest.

If we are worth anything, it is not because we have more money or more talent, or more human qualities. Insofar as we are worth anything, it is because we are grafted onto Christ's life, his cross and resurrection. That is a person's measure.

The transcendence that the church preaches is not alienation. It is not going to heaven to think about eternal life and forget about the problems on earth, it is transcendence from the human heart.

It is entering into the reality of a child, of the poor, of those wearing rags, of the sick, of a hovel, of a shack. It is going to share with them. And from the very heart of misery, of this situation, to transcend it, to elevate it, to promote it, and to say to them, 'You aren't trash. You aren't marginalized. It is to say exactly the opposite, you are valuable.'

There are not two categories of people. There are not some who were born to have everything and leave others with nothing and a majority that has nothing and can't enjoy the happiness that God has created for all. God wants a Christian society, one in which we share the good things that God has given for all of us.

It is not enough to be good. It is not enough to not do evil. My Christianity is something more positive; it is not a negative. There are many who say, 'But I don't kill, I don't steal, I don't do anything bad to anyone.' That's not enough. You are still lacking a great deal. It is not enough to be good. There are many things that can only be seen through eyes that have cried." (emphasis added)

Like Jesus, Romero was killed not because of the words he spoke but because he translated his words into action. It was that action which inspired others to live out his words. Several years ago I met a woman from Romero's town. I asked her what happened as a result of his murder. She said the faith of the people was enhanced. They saw a person who not only spoke the truth but was willing to live by that truth and even die for it. Such a truth cannot be killed. Recently he was beatified by the Catholic Church. The night before the ceremony thousands of people gathered in an all-night to celebrate his life, his death and his beatification.

It is not only religious leaders who can speak words of peace, words of justice. President John Kennedy spoke similar words: "Mankind must put an end to war, or war will put an end to mankind. War will exist until that distant day when the conscientious objector enjoys the same reputation and prestige that the warrior does today. Written in Chinese, the word crisis is composed of two characters. One represents danger and the other represents opportunity. If a free society cannot help the many who are poor, it cannot save the few who are rich. Let us resolve to be masters, not the victims, of our history, controlling our own destiny without giving way to blind suspicions and emotions.

And is not peace, in the last analysis, basically a matter of human rights—the right to live out our lives without fear of devastation—the right to breathe air as nature provided it—the right of future generations to a healthy existence?"

The world is very different now. For man holds in his mortal hands the power to abolish all forms of human poverty and all forms of human life. And yet the same revolutionary beliefs for which our forebears fought are still at issue around the globe—the belief that the rights of man come not from the generosity of the state, but from the hand of God. We dare not forget today that we are the heirs of that first revolution. Let the word go forth from this time and place, to friend and foe alike, that the torch has been passed to a new generation of Americans—born in this century, tempered by war, disciplined by a hard and bitter peace, proud of our ancient heritage—and unwilling to witness or permit the slow undoing of those human rights to which this Nation has always been committed, and to which we are committed today at home and around the world.

To those peoples in the huts and villages across the globe struggling to break the bonds of mass misery, we pledge our best efforts to help them help themselves, for whatever period is required—not because the Communists may be doing it, not because we seek their votes, but because it is right. If a free society cannot help the many who are poor, it cannot save the few who are rich. But neither can two great and powerful groups of nations take comfort from our present course—both sides overburdened by the cost of modern weapons, both rightly alarmed by the steady spread of the deadly atom, yet both racing to alter that uncertain balance of terror that stays the hand of mankind's final war. Let both sides explore what problems unite us instead of belaboring those problems which divide us. Let both sides, for the first time, formulate serious and precise proposals for the inspection and control of arms—and bring the absolute power to destroy other nations under the absolute control of all nations. Let both sides seek to invoke the wonders of science instead of its terrors. Together let us explore the stars, conquer the deserts, eradicate disease, tap the ocean depths, and encourage the arts and commerce. And so, my fellow Americans: ask not what your country can do for you—ask what you can do for your country. My fellow citizens of the world: ask not what America will do for you, but what together we can do for the freedom of man. Finally, whether you are citizens of America or citizens of the world, ask of us the same high standards of strength and sacrifice which we ask of you. With a good conscience our only sure reward, with history the final judge of our deeds, let us go forth to lead the land we love, asking His blessing and His help, but knowing that here on earth God's work must truly be our own."

John Kennedy was murdered. Despite words and actions, his legacy was quite different: prolonged war in Vietnam, expanded arms race, increasing national debt, continual war. To proclaim a legacy cannot guarantee it will be lived.

Then there is the legacy of Adolph Hitler.

Hitler lived in a Germany which had been suppressed. Its currency was worthless. Almost a wheelbarrow of money was necessary to purchase a loaf of bread. Instead of uniting people to seek a common solution to their problem, Hitler divided people and nations against one another.

Instead of a legacy of one world, one people united in a common cause and a common hope, Hitler attempted to create a master race. Because they were a master race they had a right to kill others for no other reason than they were not members of that master race. Its scientists had united in a mutual effort to create weapons and gasses which killed masses of people.

Hitler and the structures he helped spawn were defeated but their legacy continues. IG Farben created the gas which killed so many people in German concentration camps. Other scientists created bombs, gasses which killed vast numbers of people beside those in concentration camps. At the end of the war IG Farben was split into four corporations that continued to make destructive gasses, which attempt to break down the natural processes of food production. Among them were the scientists who were working to create a super bomb and were sent to other lands where the process not only continued but expanded. At any time an egotistical maniac in the wrong place could devastate much, if not all of the world.

The basic legacy left by Hitler was a legacy of fear. That same fear has led to the arms race, the huge debt now devastating many nations. The huge expenditures on military and weapons have meant less money for the ordinary needs of people.

This book will look a little more in depth at the extent of that legacy but more importantly at some of the solutions ordinary people are employing today to counteract the legacy of fear, violence, and hatred.

Postwar Development of IG Farben

Many are aware of "The Holocaust" and IG Farben's role in that holocaust. Many are not aware that several other German corporations also participated in adding victims to the holocaust. The greatest share of the blame seems to fall of Adolph Hitler. It is certainly not the intention of this author to in any way exonerate Hitler. But again, there is a very simple truth we may overlook. Hitler is gone. IG Farben is very much alive. It has been split into four separate corporations - corporations which were originally corporate members of IG Farben. Several executives of these corporations were condemned at Nuremberg. Within a few years their prison sentences were commuted and they were back heading their corporations. Although IG Farben was shut down very soon after World War Two in August 1950. Its stock was not taken from the German stock market until August, 2011. cf. dw.de

In the 1930's IG Farben transferred some of its technology to General Aniline, a corporation based in the USA. In 1942 after the USA entered World War Two the USA took over control of General Aniline still using technology from IG Farben who continued to keep some of its top executives at General Aniline even when it came under USA control. IG Farben assigned many of its patents to General Aniline so it was able to continue producing the various elements it had been producing. One of these products was carbonyl iron powder, used for military purposes. Research discoveries at General Aniline and Film were sent to IG Farben for their use. IG Farben had an exclusive selling agent, GDC. It continued to charge 15% on all material sold by General Aniline and Film. General Aniline and Film was seized by the Government of the USA which also seized GDC. Initially General Aniline had the initials IG in its name. In 1939 IG Farben dropped the initials IG from General Aniline and renamed the company General Aniline and Film. Previously, the owner had been listed as IG Chemie, a Swiss Corporation which actually was a subsidiary of Farben.

In December, 1945 The U. S. Senate Subcommittee of the Committee on Military Affairs for the U. S. Senate issued a report on IG Farben and its war effort. It stated among many things: IG Farben's external assets were "far flung and carefully camouflaged". The information they used came from IG Farben's records and from the Committee's interrogation of IG Farben's leaders. There are 2 versions of the report. The second is shorter and its opening section states some of the material from the initial report "cannot be made public because of the possible prejudice which might result to the interest of the Government." Op.cit. Preface. No indication what the "possible prejudice" might be.

The report begins with a summary which concludes that IG Farben had its own dream of a world empire. This dream was expressed in a June, 1940 document, "Neuordning" (New Order). In that document Farben lists three objectives to implement this New Order:

1 "insure the full cooperation of the conquered nations in producing for the Wehrmacht" (armed forces of Germany of Hitler's new world order).

2 ""Eliminate United States competition in the world market"

3 "utilize its vaunted economic warfare weapons, cartels, capital investment and know how in anticipation of a possible conflict between Germany and the United States."

The summary of the Report says "Even prior to Nazi conquest, IG was the major chemical firm on the Continent." It lists the value of the acquired chemical and dyestuff firms in conquered nations at approximately RM 350,000,000. (about $11,400 billion in U.S currency today.) IG also absorbed major chemical firms. It also mentions that by building new war plants in the conquered nations IG increased its capital investments by approximately RM700,000,000 ($22,800 billion in U.S. today) The summary concludes: "IG so increased the technical dependence of industry in the conquered nations that despite German defeat it can regain its position of control" (emphasis added) The summary ends with a quote from Dr. Van Schneider: "Thus I must conclude that IG is largely responsible for Hitler's policy." Ibid. Summary.

SUMMARY

More than 30 years earlier the U. S. Congress investigated the banking industry in the United States. The investigation revealed that eighteen firms investigated by the committee held 385 directorships in forty-one banks and trust companies, with total resources of $3,832,000,000 and total deposits of $2,834,000,000, fifty directorship in eleven insurance companies having total assets of $2,646,000,000; 155 directorships in thirty-one railroad systems having a total capitalization of $12,193,000,000 and a total mileage of 163,200; six directorships in two express companies and four directorships in one steamship company with a combined capital of $245,000,000 and gross income of $97,000,000; ninety-eight directorships in twenty-eight producing and trading companies having a total capitalization of $3,353,000,000 and total gross annual earnings in excess of $1,145,000,000; and forty-eight directorships in nineteen public utility corporations having a total capitalization of $3,583,000,000 and total gross annual earnings in excess of $1,145,000,000; and forty-eight directorships in nineteen public utility corporations having a total capitalization of $2,826,000,000 and total gross annual earnings in excess of $428,000,000. These eighteen firms had a total of 746 directorships in 134 corporations and total resources or capitalization of $25,325,000,000. Cf. US Congress House Committee on Finance re Pujo Report 1913

A recurring question in the investigation was whether corporate entities should be subject to U.S. Government oversight. This was not a recommendation of the Committee. Another question raised by the investigation is: This investigation eventually helped create a bill from the U.S. Congress to create the Federal Reserve Bank? There seems to be little evidence that the Federal Reserve Bank was created because of this investigation. However, it seems apparent that little was learned from this investigation. 100 years after the Federal Reserve was created there is still no federal oversight of the books of the Federal Reserve Bank.

In Europe there was IG Farben, in the U.S.A. the banks. Is there any way these two can be combined? The answer to that question came at the end of World War Two. IG benefited financially from the war, the nation of Germany was in debt and held responsible for much e damage caused by the war.t Farben was not held responsible for any debt from World War 1. But Farben was a chief economic benefactor of the war.

The conclusion reached by the Pujo Committee quoted above is found in my book <u>Why We Are Always Broke</u> (cf. op. cit. chapter 6). Immediately after that, the same book details the working of the Bank for International Settlements. After World War Two, IG Farben was "broken up" - at least that was what the public was told. Actually IG Farben was splintered in several parts. Each part was headed by one of the major elements of IG Farben: BASF, Bayer, Hoecht, and Agfa.

The major legacy left by the skeletons of IG Farben was not weapons or petroleum. It was the economic trust it left in the USA. Their USA bank trust had been consolidated into the U.S. Federal Reserve Bank which by now was the central bank of the USA. The solution of the skeletons of Farben was to unite the Federal Reserve Bank and the Bank for International Settlements. This task had been simplified because IG Farben had already established deep roots in corporations, banks, and individuals who created the Federal Reserve Bank. This is brought out in <u>Why We Are Always Broke</u>.

A common perception is Hitler was responsible for and the main agitator of World War Two. But Hitler is dead and the skeletons of IG Faben remain and often (cf. later in this book) continue in the same direction as IG Farben. We are also led to believe that the League of Nations (founded after World War One) was a failure. The League of Nations was dissolved. The court that set it up is gone. Very few persons know it helped to create a Bank, the Bank for International Settlements, which still exists today and has become the central bank for the world.

Chapter six of <u>Why We Are Always Broke</u> has a section on the Bank for International Settlements. Few people even know the bank exists. Over several years I visited several large libraries in doing research for <u>Why We Are Always Broke</u>. I looked through the index of books in the economic sections of these libraries (a thousand or more books). Not a single one had a section on the Bank for International Settlements. Very few even had a reference to it.

My analysis of the bank was very short. But it reveals several important points: 1. The bank is needed for the benefit of large bankers rather than for the needs of the general population. 2. The bank has been a leading force in the creation of an international monetary system that is completely immune from any government oversight. 3. A major function of the bank is to promote a one world economy.

Eighty years ago Eleanor Dulles wrote a book about the bank: <u>The Bank for International Settlements at Work</u>. The book was very favorable to the bank. In searching many libraries, it was the only book I could find about the bank. There were three things which caused me to question the legitimacy of the book: 1. It was written before the workings of the bank were really known. 2. The bank then, as now, did not allow their operations to be subject to external scrutiny. 3. Two of her brothers (Allen and John Foster) were important forces in setting up the bank.

In 2013 Adam Lebor was the first person to publish an in depth book on the Bank for International Settlements (<u>Towel of Basel</u>). When I first heard the title I read it as a comparison of the Bank for International Settlements and the Tower of Babel from the book of <u>Genesis</u> in the Bible. When I first saw the book with a picture of the building which houses the bank and the subtitle: "<u>The Shadowy History of the Secret Bank That Runs The World</u>" I was sure of the connection. The Tower of Babel was never completed because its builders were unable to communicate with one another.

Lebor brings out in his book the very clear truth that the builders of the Tower of Basel have lost their ability to communicate with the world or even to understand the message they are communicating to one another and to the rest of the world. They are trying to control just as the builders of Babel did. Labor also builds a strong case that this ability to communicate will bring down the Tower of Basel as surely as it brought down the Tower of Babel.

Lebor predicts that despite its power and influence Basel is as susceptible to falling as was Babel. He lists certain flaws which will bring about that fall. 1. The basic contradiction of the bank is that it calls for strict confidentiality for itself but claims to be regulating the future of other banks. 2. The bank is not needed. 3. Banks like the Bundesbank which was forced to accept euros from the Eurobank, created in part by the Bank for International Settlements is now looking more to use gold.

Finally, most persons have never even heard of the Bank for International Settlements. As the financial crisis deepens, more and more people will become aware of the Bank for International Settlements. Lebor calls this its "Achilles heel". For anyone attempting to understand the Bank for International Settlements, Tower of Basel is a very valuable tool.

The report lists four major areas of concentration: 1. "To restrict German economic penetration outside the borders of the Reich." 2. "To prevent Germany from sequestering assets outside Germany." 3. "To assure that German assets would be available for postwar reparations of Europe." 4. "To prevent the escape of those members of the Nazi ruling elite who had been marked down for war crimes trials." The State Department eventually became "principally responsible" for setting up SAFEHAVEN. State invited the formal participation of the Organization of Strategic Services (OSS). The OSS brought in its Secret Intelligence unit (SI) and its Counterintelligence unit, X-2. Germany still needed material to carry on the war but was less able to buy these items with Reich marks. Switzerland became an important source for converting Reich marks into other currencies and into gold. The OSS contact in Switzerland was Allen Dulles who had 'extensive ties to European banking interests including Thomas McKittrick, head of the Bank for International Settlements. The report also states Dulles was "unwilling" to give SAFEHAVEN the attention it warranted. According to a CIA memo quoted in the report, "Dulles looked forward to a postwar settlement that envisioned the United States working closely with European business and banking circles to reshape Western and Central Europe according to American interests." (emphasis added)

Dulles became head of the Central Intelligence Agency (CIA). He was responsible for the Bay of Pigs invasion of Cuba. He was fired by President Kennedy for that activity. He was a main (some say THE main) force in defining the Warren Commission Report on JFK's death Kennedy shot by a "lone assassin"

X2 reported the following: 1. gold and bonds looted by the Nazis from all over Europe and received by certain Swiss banks 2. Funds sent by the Deutsche Verkehrs-Kreditbank of Karlsruhe to Basel. 3. Securities held in Zurich by private firms for the Nazi Party. 4. Large quantities of Swiss francs credited to private accounts in various Swiss banks. 5. Money and property held in Liechtenstein. 6. More than 2 million francs held by the Reich bank in Switzerland. 7. 45 million Reich marks held in covert Swiss bank accounts.

According to the report the material was brought in by "German and Swiss banks and business agencies." The methods used were "smuggling, diplomatic pouches, undercover exchanges of foreign currencies, Swiss bank accounts and trusts, sales of paintings and other valuables, and the black market." In my research I frequently came across references to the Nazis looting paintings and art objects and wondered how that fit into the picture.

At the end of the war Switzerland had received (by Allied estimate) $781-$785 million in Nazi gold. $579 million came from Nazi aggression. Switzerland could do little to prevent the Allies from forcing them to pay part of the reparation debt because they profited from that activity. In the end they were only asked to pay $58 million. The advent of the "Cold War" shifted attention away from the Nazi debt. The Bank for International Settlements was the largest channel for gold transfers in prewar and wartime Europe.

When did the "cold war" begin? What was its cause? When I looked up the advent of the "cold war" on the internet I found many events listed as the cause of the "cold war". The war in Europe ended four months before my ninth birthday. I remember I had a deck of cards. They did not have the symbols usually found on playing cards. Instead there were airplanes which had the flags of various nations. At the bottom of the page was the name of the nation. I took the cards and separate the "good guys" (Allies) from the "bad guys"(Nazis)

I wasn't sure on which side to put the Russian plane. I asked my mother and she told that for now they were on our side but once the war would end "who knows?" I was not a particularly astute child. I certainly had little sense of the rest of the world. My world was limited to the range of my tricycle. That range was further limited by the range of my mother's voice. Outside that range my only knowledge came from what I heard on the radio or what I heard adults say. I bring this up simply to state that regardless of what event or even series of events that triggered the "cold war" there was an inherent mistrust of the Russians - even when they were our allies.

Some of the "causes" of the "cold war" were Stalin's statement that capitalism and communism could never coexist, the Berlin Wall, Soviet violations of treaties and other causes. Arthur Schlesinger Jr. wrote an article in Foreign Affairs entitled Origins of the Cold War. In the article he attempts to give some new insights into the origin of "cold war". He mentions, for example that the Allied leaders were all older men in their 70's and had seen a lot of attempts by one nation to take over another.

op. cit. Vol 46 no. 1 (Oct. 1961) pp. 22-52

One of his prime examples is Poland. World War Two was triggered by Germany invading Poland. When the Soviet Union took over Poland the Allies saw this as a repeat of the Nazis taking over Poland. They also viewed Poland as the home of Auschwitz site of much of the holocaust. However, Schlesinger suggests that the Soviet Union saw it in a different light. They had been invaded several times. Each invasion was launched from Poland. Western Allies viewed Soviet action as aggression. The Soviets saw it as self- protection (national security). Ibid.

One was controlled by the Soviets, the others by the USA and its Allies. John Foster Dulles and other Americans rejected the "sphere of influence" concept. In their minds that concept had already broken down. On the other hand, Great Britain had gone to war with Germany because it invaded Poland. She could not end the war by allowing Russia to invade Poland.

Despite giving a new interpretation of events believed to cause World War Two, Schlesinger ends the article by saying it was the inflexibility of Stalin which brought on the war. Even if we eliminate the events which normally we regard as causing the war, it is still persons which cause war and other tragedies.

The major reason is that human beings interpret the actions of others with their own mindset.

I agree with Schlesinger on that point. However I have read enough of Schlesinger's works to know he also has a mindset he uses to interpret human history. That mindset puts actions of Government in a supreme position and downplays the actions of industry and banks.

The Soviet Union has broken down. Because USA fought Communism wherever it broke out, the USA has amassed a huge debt, our internal structures are grossly in need of repair, many of our people live in poverty but IG Farben is stronger than it ever was during World War Two. What is the heritage of IG Farben?

IG Farben was divided into four distinct corporations: BASF. Bayer, Hoescht. and AGFA. All still exist nearly 70 years after IG Farben was dissolved. Some of the IG Farben children have been annexed or absorbed by other corporations. All of them still exist and are individually larger than the entire IG Farben ever was. We will look at the remnant of IG Farben in a later section of this book.

IG Farben is mentioned frequently as the home of Auschwitz and the producer of Zyklon B, a major drugs used to exterminate people in the holocaust. At least two books (Dr. David Picking Hitler's Table Talk and David Irving The German Atomic Bomb) state that even as Germany's defeat was apparent, Hitler was talking about a "secret weapon" which would turn the tide on the war. That weapon was the atomic bomb. Some, including the two mentioned above, suggest it was to be produced at Auschwitz.

Information available from U.S. Government documents

Pressure came from the USA and from very divergent groups to bomb this center where prisoners were detained and killed. They were always turned down. The recurring argument was such an effort would divert military forces from their central mission. Eventually in late summer 1944 the area around Auschwitz was bombed but the death camp was spared. This would give some credence to the work of Dr. Picking and Mr. Irving.

Since 1939 German scientists had been working to build an atomic bomb. It is hard to believe that the scientists at IG Farben were not aware of this. They and other German groups were using Zyklon B at the time of their mass extermination projects. What is it about IG Farben that makes it so immune from any outside oversight?

In looking at different books, articles, and other material about Hitler, IG Farben, and the holocaust I was always confused whether blame for the holocaust lay principally with I. G. Farben or with Hitler. While I could definitely see that Hitler was to blame, I realized that he alone could not have pulled off the horrors of World War Two. I found a quote by Peter Hayes in his book Industry and Ideology: IG Farben in the Nazi Era (2nd edition):

> "Nazi economic policy rested on the recognition that so long as the state not only displays its determination but permits businessmen to make money they will let themselves be manipulated as to how." (q.v. p 379) The quote seems to imply Hitler was manipulator and Farben allowed itself to be manipulated I order to make more money. It is true Hitler had a role in the decision and actions of Farben. We need to look at what the "children" of IG Farben do today. They still help produce chemicals which kill large numbers of people e.g. Agent Orange.

Certainly the State showed no determination to save lives. Today, where is the state displaying its determination not to kill vast amounts of people? There IS still a huge profit to be made in the process of killing. What is common to Germany under Hitler and our 21st Century USA is the desire to control. As long as businessmen are allowed to create chemicals and other agents to kill and politicians can control by any means they choose, we will have an IG Farben.

Hayes also stated the Nazis used the economic condition of the day to help them rise to power. That is true. For example, the Wall Street crash of 1929 did not just affect the economy of the world. The Treaty of Versailles a few years earlier mandated that Germany pay for the harm it caused in World War One and the debts it incurred. Germany was in no position to pay those debts mandated by Versailles. The U.S.A. was loaning money to Germany so she could pay those debts. With the collapse of the U.S. economy, Germany was no longer able to pay her debts.

Even while the U.S. Government was unable to aid Germany, U.S. Corporations were assisting the Nazis. Many U.S. major corporations did business with Nazi Germany before and after U.S. involvement in World War Two. This is documented in U.S. Government investigations and the research of several writers. No serious penalties have been inflicted on these corporations.

Nazi invasion of Poland is usually seen as the starting point of World War Two. Prior to the end of World War One parts of Poland were under the control of Germany. The treaty of Versailles stripped Germany of that control. One Polish area allowed German access to a vital port so Germany could export its goods. We are so quick to relate world events to political decisions and so slow to recognize the economic consequences of political decisions.

Despite the poor economic status of Germany, IG Farben and its leaders were building an economic empire. It had developed a satellite company in the USA, General Aniline and Film, as well as IG Chemie of Switzerland. It set up a special organization, Chemnyco, Inc., of New York. IG participated in the plunder of conquered countries (Austria, Czechoslovakia, Poland, Norway, Holland, Belgium, France and all the rest of Central Europe), seizing their factories and taking them over. There was an operation within Argentina of subsidiaries of Germany's leading firms, including I.G. Farben. They set up major espionage centers for the Nazis.

After World War Two, General Eisenhower was commander of the U. S. Army and Allies. He ordered an investigation of the role IG Farben played in the success of the Nazis. The report concluded Farben was indispensable to the German effort. As a result of the report Eisenhower decided to

1. make I.G. plants and other assets available for reparations;
2. destroy I.G. plants used exclusively for war making purposes;
3. break up I.G.'s monopoly control by dispersing ownership of the remaining plants;
4. terminate I.G.'s interest in international cartels;
5. take over I.G.'s research programs and facilities.

IG Farben was "liquidated" two times - once according to the decrees of the Allied Powers who occupied Germany. The second by the West German Government once it was formally established as the official government of West Germany. In both cases the advisory group which oversaw the process was composed of former Farben officials. IG Farben was the second largest stockholder in Standard Oil. I.G. Farben also owned stock in other U. S. corporations which backed them.

Eisenhower witnessed the full impact of I.G. Farben. He experienced the horrors of war, the difficulty in attempting to seek peace as well the forces which profit from war and struggle. He became president of the United States for eight years. In his final address to the U.S. Congress he warned:

"Until the latest of our world conflicts, the United States had no armaments industry. American makers of plowshares could, with time and as required, make swords as well. But now we can no longer risk emergency improvisation of national defense; we have been compelled to create a permanent armaments industry of vast proportions. Added to this, three and a half million men and women are directly engaged in the defense establishment. We annually spend more on military security than the net income of all United States corporations. -

This conjunction of an immense military establishment and a large arms industry is new in the American experience. The total influence -- economic, political, even spiritual -- is felt in every city, every State house, every office of the Federal government.

We recognize the imperative need for this development. Yet we must not fail to comprehend its grave implications. Our toil, resources and livelihood are all involved; so is the very structure of our society.

In the councils of government, we must guard against the acquisition of unwarranted influence, whether sought or unsought, by the military industrial complex. The potential for the disastrous rise of misplaced power exists and will persist." (Farewell Address of President Eisenhower to U. S. Congress Jan. 17, 1961)

Many persons remember Eisenhower's military years as well as the eight years he spent as President of the United States. Only a few are aware that for almost five years he was President of Columbia University. These were years when a great transition began to occur in education. Few remember Eisenhower's next words after warning of the military industrial complex. These words reflect his experience as President of Columbia University: "Akin to, and largely responsible for the sweeping changes in our industrial-military posture, has been the technological revolution during recent decades. In this revolution, research has become central; it also becomes more formalized, complex, and costly. A steadily increasing share is conducted for, by, or at the direction of, the Federal government.

Today, the solitary inventor, tinkering in his shop, has been overshadowed by task forces of scientists in laboratories and testing fields. In the same fashion, the free university, historically the fountainhead of free ideas and scientific discovery has experienced a revolution in the conduct of research. Partly because of the huge costs involved, a government contract becomes virtually a substitute for intellectual curiosity. For every old blackboard there are now hundreds of new electronic computers.

The prospect of domination of the nation's scholars by Federal employment, project allocations, and the power of money is ever present and is gravely to be regarded. Yet, in holding scientific research and discovery in respect, as we should, we must also be alert to the equal and opposite danger that public policy could itself become the captive of a scientific technological elite" (Ibid)

For Eisenhower both dangers are related. Both create an elite group which is powerful, costly and removed from the influence of ordinary people. I have read speculation that "military industrial complex" was a reference to the dangers of another I. G. Farben. I will not attempt to prove or disprove that theory. However, he saw first-hand widespread consequences of IG Farben and spoke as a warning to us all how we could develop our own IG Farben or even worse how IG Farben and its heirs could lead us to another holocaust.

Europe was quickly rebuilt after World War Two and continued to advance in the 70 years since the war ended. Europe now has a single currency, the euro. There is even talk of a possible single government of Europe. Structures damaged by war can easily be rebuilt. Some even suggest war is good. It creates jobs. I remember a neighbor back in the days World War Two was winding down saying she hoped the war would continue. It gave her a job she might lose when the war ended.

There are other consequences of war we may not notice. War destroys the people who survive the war. It often shatters the dreams of people, especially young people who represent a very large portion of those who actually fight the wars. In war a person can go out and kill large numbers of other human beings and then be considered a hero for doing so. Such actions create an indelible scar on a person's psyche.

In war, our own soldiers inhale the toxic gas they spread to kill other people. Then our leaders try to pretend there is no connection between the diseases and maladies they have with having subjected themselves to the poisons they have spread. Destructive drugs often accompany a veteran returning from war. Again, our leaders try to deny any responsibility. Sometimes those addictive drugs are the only tool a soldier has to help justify killing other people and being isolated in a foreign environment.

We seem to forget, or at least ignore, the fact that persons killed in war had some hobby, some dream which could have impelled that person to do something that would have been useful to humanity. The dead person was a brother or sister, child or parent, father or mother, a spouse. Making that person a statistic, an anonymous hero we remember on Memorial Day, will not repair the damage to the many psyches affected by this death.

Even if we remember and experience the damage done to the families of our own heroes, we rarely recognize that the same scars were created in the families of our enemies who died. Among the many millions who have died in the wars during our own lifetime would there not be at least one who found a cure for cancer or some other great benefit to humanity? How many great authors were killed, how many great teachers, great religious leaders?

We have taken the personal element out of war and the deaths they cause. We seem to forget that wars are profitable for people who create the weapons and other supplies needed in warfare. We also seem to ignore the fact that wars are possible because we remain silent. We end with a quote from Merchants of death by H. C. Engelbrecht and F. C. Hanighen:

> "The arms industry did not create the war system. On the contrary, the war system created the arms industry.... All constitutions in the world invest the war-making power in the government or in the representatives of the people. The root of the trouble, therefore, goes far deeper than the arms industry. It lies in the prevailing temper of peoples toward nationalism, militarism, and war, In the civilization which forms this temper and prevents any drastic and radical change. Only when this underlying basis of the war system is altered, will war and its concomitant, the arms industry, pass out of existence."

> Wars don't just happen (cf. following chart). Wars are created by human action. In this book we will look at the actions of Russia and the USA. We will also look at the role played by the remnant of Nazis who pledged themselves to continue the mission of Nazism by continuing to divide nations and keep them at war.

US Military Intelligence report EW-Pa 128
Source: INTELLIGENCE REPORT NO. EW-Pa 128

SUPREME HEADQUARTERS
ALLIED EXPEDITIONARY FORCE
Office of Assistant Chief of Staff, G-2
7 November 1944

Some of the major points in the report: "German industry must realize that the war cannot be won and that it must take steps for a post war commercial campaign." (emphasis added) Success of this campaign will help lay "the financial tool for borrowing considerable sums of money from foreign countries.' This money is to be "at the disposal of the party"

-16-

Some of the money will be used to create bureaus which "will receive plans and drawings of new weapons **as well as documents which they need to continue their research and which must not be allowed to fall into the hands of the enemy/"** (emphasis added)

My Comment: This book will show how this German plan has been implemented. Nazi scientists were sent to other nations especially USA and Russia to help create destructive weapons and gasses many created by the remnants of IG Farben. Although not considered in this book I wonder what role Nazi remnants had in the thousands of nuclear weapons created.

"German industrials ... are placing their funds abroad, particularly in neutral countries. Two main banks through which this export of capital operates are Basler Handelsbank and the Schweizerische."

My addition: Both were foreign banks. Both pleaded guilty to holding Nazi gold, sending millions of dollars off shore to help rich clients avoid taxes. They also had insured Jews prior to any mention of the Marshall Plan which was an attempt to counteract Soviet expansion in Europe It would be difficult to prove or disprove this position. What seems apparent is it did divide East and West. What is clear is there were elements which called for unification of Europe and part of the justification for that was to enhance U.S. trade. I have not found any U.S. literature which addresses possible connection between the Nazi plan and the Marshall Plan. Maybe the authors of: the Marshal Plan were unaware of this plan.

The State Department officials were a major part of drafting and promoting the Marshall Plan. Both plans center on a post war Europe. Both are conceived by military persons who played a vital role in Europe during the war. Both focused on the protection of European (especially German) industry. Both looked to an expansion of influence. In fact, the USA has lived out (intentionally or unintentionally) the aim of the Nazi plan – the spread of its influence world-wide.

The Heritage of IG Farben

After World War Two, IG Farben was shut down. It was "split" into four parts - at least that is what we were told. The four parts were the four major corporations which made up IG Farben. They all continue manufacturing chemicals. Some of these chemicals are as deadly as those used in World War Two exterminations. In the wake of IG Farben and Nazi cruelty, The United States generated two major responses: SAFEHAVEN and PROJECT PAPERCLIP. These two responses helped prepare the way for the COLD WAR and the formation of the CIA. This chapter looks at SAVE HAVEN, PROJECT PAPERCLIP, the COLD WAR.

SOURCE: Agent of French Deuxieme Bureau, recommended by Commandant Zindel. This agent is regarded as reliable and has worked for the French on German problems since 1916. He was in close contact with the Germans, particularly industrialists, during the occupation of France and he visited Germany as late as August, 1944.

SAFEHAVEN

In researching and writing <u>Why We are Always Broke</u> I have believed and taken the position that we need to interpret wars and other human events in economic terms e.g. WHO benefitted from the war? I never dreamed I would obtain material on the CIA website to support of such a claim. Then I came across this document: "<u>The OSS and Project SAFEHAVEN: Tracking Nazi "Gold"</u> by Donald P. Steary. This had the seal of and bore the CIA title. I found the document listed with others by Mr. Steary. One of them identified Mr. Steary as a member of the CIA historical staff.

The report lists four major aims of SAFEHAVEN. 1 To restrict German economic penetration outside the borders of the Reich. 2 To prevent Germany from sequestering assets in neutral countries. 3 To ensure that German assets would be available for postwar reparations and the rebuilding of Europe. 4 To prevent the escape of those members of the Nazi ruling elite who had already been marked down for war crimes trials.

From: *US and Allied Efforts to Recover and Restore Gold and Other Assets Stolen or Hidden by Germany During World War II (The Eizenstat Report), Preliminary Study (May 1997), p. 15.*

The Eisenstat Report was the result of hearings in early 1997. It reported deceit on the part of the Swiss banks and implicit approval by USA. His summary includes that there was a huge amount of this gold in Swiss banks. The banks first tried to deny it but eventually admitted to receiving looted gold. Some Nazi gold was sent abroad.

Prepared Testimony of Ambassador Stuart E. Eizenstat, Under Secretary for International Trade United States Department of Commerce Senate Banking, Housing and Urban Affairs Committee 10:00 a.m., Thursday, May 15, 1997

The report also states: "It is quite clear that SAFEHAVEN planners had a good idea of what they wanted to achieve, but it also is apparent that they did not have the slightest idea of how to do it. In fact, the inception of SAFEHAVEN meant little more than a redirection of intelligence assets already dedicated to the collection of economic intelligence. The OSS had been collecting economic intelligence similar to that acquired by SAFEHAVEN since 1942 as a part of the general effort to understand the functioning of the German war economy.

Gold transfers in particular were a key part of that economy. Germany suffered from an acute shortage of certain key strategic resources since the proclamation of the Four-Year Plan and the onset of autarky (economic self-sufficiency) in 1936, the German armaments industry increasingly had to resort to specie payments or barter agreements to pay for imports of these materials since before the outbreak of the war. Conquest of Europe had done little to alleviate most of these shortages.

Moreover, due to the inefficiency of the Nazi regime--full mobilization for war production had not been achieved until 1944--the war production index for that year was nearly three times that of 1941, a significant increase over 1939-40.

Paradoxically, therefore, the German appetite for oil, high-grade iron ore, wolfram (tungsten ore), and other strategic materials grew insatiably, even as German industry reeled under the onslaught of the Allied strategic bombing campaign and the territory under German control shrank.

In their search for war materials Nazi leaders extended their net throughout Europe. High-grade iron ore and copper was imported from Sweden; iron ore from Poland, Austria, and Spain; wolfram from Portugal and Spain; chromium from Turkey. Voluntarily or involuntarily, every nation in Europe fed the German war machine with the raw materials it needed. Switzerland was the central connecting link.

Swiss cooperation had become essential as other neutrals responded to Allied pressure and refused to exchange war materials for specie. As defeat loomed, neutrals also became increasingly reluctant to accept payment in Reichsmarks. This left payment in foreign currency, of which Nazi Germany had precious little after nearly a decade of attacks and war.

In this critical situation, the Swiss banks acted as clearinghouses whereby German gold--much of which was looted from occupied countries--could be converted to a more suitable medium of exchange. An intercepted Swiss diplomatic cable shows how, allegedly without inquiring as to its origin, the Swiss National Bank helped the German Reichsbank convert some $15 million in (probably) looted Dutch gold into liquid assets:

> In May 1943 (the Swiss National Bank) sold to the Turkish CENTRAL BANK 256 bars (of gold) amounting to 14.8 million francs, which were taken over previously from the German REICHSBANK. This gold was sold back to the German REICHSBANK by the Turkish CENTRAL BANK. Later the German REICHSBANK sold 13.8 million francs of this gold to the BANCO DE PORTUGAL in Lisbon, and one million to the BANK FOR INTERNATIONAL SETTLEMENTS.

Bern #246 to Washington, 23 April 1946. Intercepted Swiss diplomatic traffic also shows that the Swiss knew that they had accepted $Fr 378,000,000 in looted Belgian gold. This gold had been deposited with the Bank of France in 1939 and was turned over to the German Government by the puppet Vichy regime. Swiss justification for this was that "the only way in which Belgian gold got into German hands was through the Laval government." Washington #256, to Bern; 25 April 1946.

To Allied observers, these covert German activities looked like a conspiracy to build an underground economy--an activity that would have profound implications for SAFEHAVEN. In fact, such efforts represented little more than the desperate attempts of the Nazi leadership to preserve access to vital sources of raw materials and had little to do with visions of a resurgent Fourth Reich. Then, too, individual Germans and German corporations were taking steps to conceal assets in foreign countries to protect them against destruction or seizure by the victorious Allied armies

A footnote reads: A fundamental error committed by the planners of SAFEHAVEN (as well as X-2) was the assumption that actions of individual German corporations and Nazi leaders of necessity represented the policy of the National Socialist regime. Although there were some attempts by parts of the regime to plan for underground activities after the war (such as the half-mythical Werwolf program), they were far less important than ever imagined by SAFEHAVEN planners. The vast bulk of the attempts to conceal wealth in foreign countries detected by SAFEHAVEN program were initiated by individuals and individual corporations anticipating the imminent collapse of the Reich.
Source: RG 226, Entry 116, Records of the Office of Strategic Services; Office of the Director, Microfilm Publication 1642, Reel 108; Murphy to Mowinckel, 4 June 1945, "X-2 Case Materials Illustrating German SAFEHAVEN Practices."

Was this fundamental error a cause of the cold war and the failure to look at IG Farben and other industries in analyzing 1945 German intentions? Was it really an error or was part of the plan?

The report continues with a look at Allen Dulles and his role at Bern. Under these circumstances, it is scarcely surprising that implementation of SAFEHAVEN measures depended largely upon personalities of the OSS chiefs of mission and the conditions under which they operated. In the heart of the Swiss banking and German gold transfer activity, the OSS chief was Allen W. Dulles, later (1953 to 1962) Director of Central Intelligence. An East Coast Brahain with extensive prewar ties to European banking circles, Dulles spent his tenure in Bern constructing an "old-boy" network of sources that extended throughout neutral and Axis-occupied Europe.

It was an astonishingly successful system, ideally suited to his situation in neutral Switzerland and well suited to gain access to European government and business circles. For example, Dulles counted among his close personal friends no less a personage than Thomas B. McKittrick, President of the Bank for International Settlements (BIS), in Basel. A multinational corporation created to manage international currency and gold exchanges. BIS was single-largest channel for gold transfers to prewar and wartime Europe. McKittrick also was an OSS source providing Dulles with "comfortable access" to thinking of the bankers most responsible for moving German assets throughout Europe. Among other information, McKittrick kept Dulles informed of the comings and goings of *Reichsbankvizepräsident* Emil Puhl, the architect of the German gold transfer arrangements. Source: RG 226, Entry 99, Box 13, Folder 41-1 OSS History Office, Cable Digest; 23 March 1945, #7387 21 March 1945, 110 (Dulles) to Washington.

Other well-placed sources available to Dulles in high European financial circles included Dr. Eduard Waetjen, Abwehr agent, member of the German resistance, and commercial adviser to the German Consul General, Maurice Villars, General Director of the Zurich Electro-Bank; and Swedish economist and

Economic Adviser to the BIS, Dr. Per Jacobsson, who was close to (the surprisingly extensive) Japanese diplomatic and business circles in Switzerland. In 1945, Jacobsson provided information that helped scuttle a Japanese attempt to buy vitally needed ball bearings in Sweden and later served with Maurice Villars as a mediator for Japanese peace feelers.

Such contacts were clearly important. It also seems clear that the high value Dulles attributed to them ... made him wary of intelligence activities such as SAFEHAVEN. Dulles looked forward to a postwar settlement that envisioned the United States working closely with European business and banking circles to reshape Western and Central Europe according to American interests. (Emphasis added)

On 28 December 1944, following receipt of the OSS memorandum regarding cooperation with United States' SAFEHAVEN project, he cabled Washington: .... Today we must fish in troubled waters and maintain contacts with persons suspected of working with Nazis on such matters.

RG 226, Entry 116, Records of the Office of Strategic Services, Office of the Director, Microfilm Publication 1642, Reel 108. Cable: Bern 2677, 28 December 1944.

Because of Dulles' decision, X-2 was up and running in Switzerland. By April it was able to provide OSS Washington with an extensive summary of Nazi gold and currency transfers arranged via Switzerland through most of the war. a footnote here states: According to X-2, there is Operation LAURA. By February 1946, X-2 was able to document quantities of gold shipped from Switzerland to the Iberian Peninsula. Unfortunately, none of the reporting appears to be preserved in covert Swiss bank accounts

CIA job 78-00323A, Box181 folder 14, Joyce from Blum X-2(Bern Progress Report link" Feb. 1948

X-2 reported only a few cases where private individuals, some of whom were believed to be with German intelligence organizations, participated. Methods used included smuggling, diplomatic pouches, undercover exchange of foreign currencies, Swiss bank accounts and trusts, sales of paintings and other valuables, and the black market

From: RG 226, Entry 116, Records of the OSS; Office of the Director, Microfilm Publication 1642, Reel 108; Murphy to Mowinckel, 4 June 1945, "X-2 Case Materials Illustrating German SAFEHAVEN Practices."

There was William Casey whose postwar vision saw the USA playing business interests in Germany against each other and against Communist and Socialist-led labor unions. He welcomed an opportunity to collect intelligence showing Nazi connections to supposedly neutral business circles in order to influence these same circles in the postwar world. So Casey launched into SAFEHAVEN with such enthusiasm that he had to be restrained by Washington in a cable (18 January 1945).

...While SAFEHAVEN has certain present and potentially greater future value, no SI personnel which can possibly be used in connection with agent penetration of Germany...should be used for any SAFEHAVEN purpose. For this project we can be one of any supporting agencies for Department of State which has assumed control and direction for agent penetration of Germany, for strategic information and for proper briefing such agents of US Government can look only to OSS SI to accomplish its characteristic mission.

from: RG 226, Entry 116, Records of the OSS, Office of the Director, Microfilm Publication 1942, Reel 108. Cable: 4174, to 908 and Casey from 154 (Shepardson) 18 January 1945.

"a massive report prepared at the request of the State Department on the activities of the Swiss firm Johann Wehrli & Co., A. G. a private Swiss banking house with global interests then under investigation by the Justice Department for its role in transferring private German assets overseas.

quote from RG 226, Entry 183, Box 21, "Wehrli combine," n.d. The economic report was based on intelligence data to complement an audit of the Wehlibank books by the US firm Price, Waterhouse & Co., conducted under joint British and American auspices.

Then there was OSS Director William Donovan. His objective was "to carve out a place for his organization in the postwar world ... SAFEHAVEN should be the starting point for large-scale and permanent economic intelligence for the protection and promotion of our economic and political interests abroad." (emphasis added)   Quote from RG 226, entry 116, Records of the OSS, Office of the Director, Microfilm Publication 1642, Reel 108. Memorandum: Donovan from George, "RE Rebuilding of German Economic, Political, and Military Power Positions Abroad by the Evasion of Allied Controls over the Exit of German Assets and Personnel from Germany (SAFEHAVEN),"

Donovan clearly saw an argument for the existence of a central intelligence organization like the OSS after the end of the war. ... Nonetheless, such action could hardly overcome the opposition that had been building to Donovan's idea of a postwar central intelligence organization since his first proposal was ventilated in September 1943.

On 20 September 1945 the OSS was abolished by Executive Order and its component parts absorbed by various agencies in the Washington bureaucracy. ... On 22 January 1946, President Truman created a temporary Central Intelligence Group (CIG) as a body for the coordination of intelligence activities on the national level.

When I was researching Why We Are Always Broke I found a letter of President Truman in the Truman Library in Independence, Missouri. The letter states Truman did not intend to create a spy agency. His intention was to create an agency that would allow him to get material he was not getting so he could make the decisions he was required to make as President.

The report goes on: "With the end of the war in Europe, first the OSS and then the SU began to shift resources away from support of the SAFEHAVEN program into other areas, especially collection against the Soviet Union. Efforts by FEA and State Department representatives in Europe to revitalize SAFEHAVEN ran up against the stone wall of budgetary limitations.

On 20 July 1945, SI Paris cabled OSS Washington:

> Original definition of SAFEHAVEN, namely tracking down German capital and assets abroad, has been very substantially broadened by (Klaus) of FEA now in Washington and Farben of Embassy, they claim under instructions of Washington. -028-

> They have asked that under SAFEHAVEN we should now gather intelligence on "external security" namely, all German activities abroad, cultural and political as well as economic and financial, in short, the entire non-military SI field of activity.... We pointed out that we were presently contracting, not expanding, our activities and that his wishes and the particular targets he was suggesting required substantial additional personnel. Quote from RG 226, entry 116, Records of the OSS, Office of the Director, Microfilm Publication 1642, Reel 108. Memorandum: Donovan from George, "RE Rebuilding of German Economic, Political, and Military Power Positions Abroad by the Evasion of Allied Controls over the Exit of German Assets and Personnel from Germany (SAFEHAVEN)," n.d., but context places it in April-June 1945.

> In my own research I found Klaus was initially named to head the team doing the investigation but General Cassius Clay wanted the military to run the search and had him replaced as head. (Cf. SAFEHAVEN: The Allied Pursuit of Nazi Assets Abroad pp.170-171)

> Noting that "We would be happy to undertake intelligence operation (of this kind) and are physically equipped to do so," Washington replied that "...no funds (are) available," and recommended that State "officially urge OSS to procure additional funds for such purposes...."
Quote from: _RG 226/Entry 134A, Box 9, Folder 26. OSS Washington #23584: Horton for Sherman from 154, 28 July 1945

No such pressure was forthcoming. To the contrary, although SAFEHAVEN remained important, with the end of the war in Europe the role of intelligence reporting in the project began to diminish. That same month, lack of Treasury and State interest prompted OSS to begin rolling up economic reporting networks in the Iberian Peninsula.
quote from: RG 226/Entry 134A, Box 9, Folder 26. Lisbon #7687: Patina from Grant and Elton, 19 July 1945; OSS Washington #8817. JETSAM. Grant and Elton from Patina, 23 July 1945.

The haste with which the USA detached its first central intelligence organization at the end of the war was replicated in Project SAFEHAVEN. As elsewhere in the government, the trend away from a general reliance on intelligence sources almost immediately reversed itself in postwar follow up to SAFE-HAVEN, as Western Allies sought to use the information collected in wartime to seek restoration of assets looted by Nazi Germany.

When I read this I realized what I had been saying: follow the money trail was correct. There was more money in pursuing reparation money than in spying. So the trail we have been led to believe was a political trail was really an economic trail. This is not info from some wild eyed liberal but is from CIA itself!

The report goes on: With virtually all of Europe economically devastated and dependent on US aid for the most basic requirements of sustenance, the Western Allies thus were presented with both the opportunity and the means to compel a general settling of accounts. Switzerland was the most obvious target.

Footnote here reads: "From Sweden, Spain, Portugal, Turkey, and Argentina, the Western Allies sought and obtained the restoration of gold and other assets looted by the Germans. These countries were, however, generally cooperative and the necessary agreements were more easily obtained."

The Swiss had profited mightily from World War II, having taken in (by Allied estimate) $781-785 million in Nazi gold, of which $579 million (or 74 percent) had been looted from the victims of Nazi aggression. Indeed, the postwar prosperity of Switzerland was based largely on the immense profits made from Nazi Germany in the war.

On the other hand, for the Swiss, the situation in the immediate postwar period was potentially dire. Having been geographically and economically isolated from non-Nazi Europe for nearly five years, the Swiss desperately need to reconstruct the export-based economy that had existed before World War II. This, in large measure, depended on the willingness of the United States and its Allies to negotiate the trade agreements necessary to sustain a viable export economy. Moreover, Switzerland was unable to feed itself and depended totally on the Allies for the imports of food and fuel it needed to survive. Thus, there was little the Swiss Government could do to prevent the Western Allies from imposing the most punitive settlement necessary to obtain the restoration of looted German gold, should they wish to do so.

In this, the Swiss were fortunate that they were negotiating with the Western Allies, not their wartime trading partners. Although the Swiss Government was haunted by fear of the economic pressure that might be imposed throughout its negotiations with the United States, at no point did the Allies make use of their position to compel an agreement. In the end the settlement negotiated with the Swiss Government fell afoul of the Cold War and the consequent shift in postwar priorities away from the problems created by Nazi Germany. The settlement ultimately reached was essentially unsatisfactory for the Allies: the Swiss agreed to a token payment of $58 million, and a 50-percent share of the value realized from liquidating German assets in Switzerland.

In addition to the intelligence collected for SAFEHAVEN, the Allies had access to the extensive files of the Reichsbank and the *Auswartiges Ämt*, the German Foreign Office. They thus had full documentation of the movement of looted German gold, and especially gold looted from the Belgian National Bank into Switzerland. The Allies were particularly indignant over an exchange of letters between the Swiss National Bank and *Reichsbankvizepräsident* Emil Puhl revealing that the Swiss had been conducting commercial negotiations with the Nazi government at the same time that they were making an agreement with the Allies to block German assets in Switzerland.

As negotiations got under way, ... Two urgent messages were dispatched from SSU Washington that month: requesting "...any possible information on instructions particularly general line of defense given Stucki," followed by a "priority" request for "...instructions to Stucki delegation re: willingness of Suisse to permit Allied seizure of German funds for reparations.... did committee have latitude for decision here?"

Petitpierre and a majority of the Swiss Federal Council had to be "convinced" that granting Allied claims to German assets was "indispensable." Petitpierre was said to be particularly concerned for the coming Swiss elections and apprehensive of a conservative reaction to Swiss resumption of diplomatic relations with the Soviet Union. On 21 March, he told the SSU source that he earnestly desired to settle "the present misunderstanding with the United States to counterbalance this gesture of friendship toward the East."

The Swiss were further prepared to accede to the demand that Allied representatives be admitted to Switzerland to track down concealed German assets, ... According to this report, the most important Swiss demand was for reimbursement for approximately SFr 500,000,000 in unpaid-for goods shipped to Germany during the war. This they planned to take from the outstanding balance of a prewar German loan for building the Gotthard Tunnel and from German investments in the Swiss railway system.

Taken from: RG 226/Entry 108A, Box 1, Folder 9. Walter S. Surrey, Esq.; Division of Economic Security Controls, Department of State from Chairman, Reporting Board SSU; 22 March 1946.

Although this intelligence was passed to State Department on 22 March, it is far from clear that it had any immediate effect on the progress of the negotiations. For a long time, the two sides were too far apart for any progress to be made. ... Moreover, the Swiss were concerned the Allies might exploit their considerable economic leverage to force them into an agreement on unfavorable terms.

It was difficult for Washington to resolve the contrast between the more flexible position on the gold issue reportedly adopted by the Swiss Foreign Office in Bern with the firm stance taken by Walther Stucki in Washington. On 27 March, SSU chief General Magruder complained to Bern, "Everything [that the] Swiss delegation has said to date," contradicted the information that had been received from the field, and requested that SSU Bern immediately confirm its previous reporting: "Much depends on it."

from: SSU Washington #WASH 2434: (Bern) BRUCC from Magruder, 27 March 1946.

Over the next two weeks negotiations became acrimonious, with both sides still far apart. ... After much discussion, on 21 May 1946 the Allies accepted Stucki's final offer.

With the conclusion of the Allied-Swiss negotiations, the files on Projects SAFEHAVEN and JETSAM were closed, and the operations themselves forgotten until, just over fifty years later, a new generation of researchers discovered them in a renewed search for "Nazi gold."

Unfortunately, none of the intelligence collected for SAFEHAVEN was useful in identifying assets that had been stolen from Jews and other victims of the Holocaust and Nazi aggression. Because of the nature of the transactions, because key records remained closed, and because the Nazis went to great lengths to conceal the origins of the gold, currencies, and other valuables transferred into neutral countries these assets were more or less anonymous until they came under the purview of SAFEHAVEN collectors.

There was voluminous reporting about transfers of gold and currency among Nazi Germany, Switzerland, Spain, Sweden, and other countries; efforts to conceal German-owned assets in neutral and nonbelligerent countries when the war ended. Attempts to transfer assets through Spain and Portugal to South America were also voluminous. Although it is nearly certain that gold and other valuables stolen from European Jews figured in these transactions but probably could never be separated from the much larger quantity of booty looted from Europe as a whole.

Nevertheless, apart from documenting the major channels of German economic activity, these findings were valuable in that they showed US secret intelligence organizations to have been assiduous in their support of US Government policy. In the final analysis, that is what is most important. A footnote explains the rationale of SAFEHAVEN *In an effort prompted by the passing of the generation chiefly victimized by the Holocaust and World War II, a team of government historians revisited the ground covered by the OSS in its efforts to track down underground sources of German industrial and commercial power. Their task was to find out what the US Government knew about Nazi efforts to exploit gold and other valuables looted from conquered countries and stolen from individual victims of the Holocaust to feed the German war effort. What they found in the SAFEHAVEN files was a mother lode of intelligence reporting on German international commercial and fiscal transactions in 1944 and 1945.*

Thus the report ends. It reveals much pertinent material e.g. the overwhelming influence of Allen Dulles on the entire process.

The report also reveals Dulles' attachment to business interests and the aim of Dulles to continue a postwar intelligence agency to promote U.S. business interests. It reveals a splintered U. S. Government idea of what response was needed. It reveals a deliberate attempt by the Government to hide information from its own people, the people most affected (the victims), and even some Government officials. It reveals military involvement in the process. What is most amazing is that the report appears on the CIA website, that it is written by one of their historians and contains their own official symbol.

One fact it does not reveal, and it cannot reveal since it is a report on SAFEHAVEN, is the role of corporations like IG Farben. On the website I found a list of more than 300 reports published by SAFEHAVEN. Only 3 even mention IG Farben. Two refer only to subsidiaries of Farben (Parke-Davis seeking a patent, Agfa transferring technical information to a Belgian film corporation.) The third is more about U. S. policy on German assets in Spain – IG Farben appears only as an example.

OPERATION PAPERCLIP

A Study of documents from The United States Secretary of State, Office of the Historian reveals the following:

OSS can be abolished by the President at any time. It was established by Presidential letter July 11, 1941, under the Office of the Coordinator of Information. On June 13, 1942 by Presidential Military Order it was renamed OSS and transferred to jurisdiction of the Joint Chiefs.

If OSS were abolished, its functions would revert to the Joint Chiefs, or to the Army and Navy separately. The present functions of OSS are (a) to collect and analyze such strategic information as may be required by the Joint Chiefs, and (b) to plan and operate such special services as may be directed by the Joint Chiefs. William Donovan, who headed the OSS, wrote the following letter to President Truman with the following attachment which he called "Statement of Policy:

"All major powers except the United States have had for a long time past permanent worldwide intelligence services, reporting directly to the highest echelons of their Governments. Prior to the present war, the United States had no foreign secret intelligence service. It never has had and does not now have a coordinated intelligence system. The defects and dangers of this situation have been generally recognized.

Adherence to the following would remedy this defect in peace as well as war so American policy could be based upon information obtained through its own sources on foreign intentions, capabilities and developments as seen and interpreted by Americans. That each Department of Government should have its own intelligence bureau for the collection and processing of such informational material as it finds necessary in the actual performance of its functions and duties. Such a bureau should be under the sole control of the Department head and should not be encroached upon or impaired by the functions granted any other Governmental intelligence agency.

Because secret intelligence covers all fields and because of possible embarrassment, no executive department should be permitted to engage in secret intelligence but in a proper case, call upon the central agency for service.

In addition to the intelligence unit for each Department there should be established a national centralized foreign intelligence agency which should have the authority:

A. To serve all Departments of the Government.

B. To procure and obtain political, economic, psychological, sociological, military and other information which may bear upon the national interest and which has been collected by the different Governmental Departments or agencies.

C. To collect when necessary supplemental information either at its own instance or at the request of any Government Department by open or secret means from other and various sources.

D. To integrate, analyze, process and disseminate to authorized to Governmental agencies and officials intelligence in the form of strategic interpretive studies. Such an agency should be prohibited from carrying on clandestine within the United States and should be forbidden the exercise of any police functions either at home or abroad.

E. Since the nature of its work requires it to have status <u>it should be independent of any Department of the Government</u> (since it is obliged to serve all and must be free of the natural bias of an operating Department). It should be under a Director, appointed by the President, and be administered under Presidential direction, or in the event of a General Manager being appointed, should be established in the Executive Office of the President, under his direction. (emphasis added)

Subject to the approval of the President or the General Manager, <u>the policy of such a service should be determined by the Director</u> with the <u>advice and assistance</u> of a Board on which the Secretaries of State, War, Navy and Treasury should be represented. (Emphasis added) note: only advice and assistance of board - not direction and control.)

That this agency, as the sole agency for secret intelligence, should be authorized in the foreign field only, to carry on services such as <u>espionage, counter-espionage and those special operations (including moral and psychological) designed to anticipate and counter any attempted penetration and subversion</u> of our national security by enemy action. (emphasis added)

Such service have an independent budget granted directly by Congress.

That it should be authorized to have its own system of codes and should be furnished facilities by Departments of Government proper and necessary for the performance of its duties.

Such a service should include in its staff specialists (within governmental Departments, civil and military, and in private life)professionally trained in analysis of information and possessing a high degree of linguistic, regional or functional competence, to analyze, coordinate and evaluate incoming information, to make special intelligence reports, and to provide <u>guidance for</u> recollecting branches of the agency.

In time of war or unlimited national emergency, all programs of such agency in areas of actual and projected military operations shall be coordinated with military plans, and shall be subject to the approval of the Joint Chiefs of Staff, or if there be a consolidation of the armed services, under the supreme commander. Parts of such programs which are to be executed in the theater of military operations shall be subject to control of the military commander.

Memorandum From the Director of the Office of Strategic Services (Donovan) to President Truman Washington, August 25, 1945.

This was the intention of the founder of the CIA. Regardless of the actual structure assigned by law, it has been the format in which it has operated. It has been an independent agency, independent of other Government agencies or persons, closely tied in to military interests, not bound by moral or psychological principles. It is to promote "national security" AS THEY DETERMINE NATIONAL SECRITY TO BE..

Operation Paperclip was the Office of Strategic Services (OSS) program in which over 1,500 German scientists, technicians, and engineers from Nazi Germany and other foreign countries were brought to the United States for employment in the aftermath of World War II. It was conducted by the <u>(JIOA), and in the context of the developing cold war.</u>

A CIA report on the Joint Intelligence Objectives Agency which was a military agency as the CIA report states: "Before the creation of the CIA, the National Security Council, or even the OSS, the American Joint Intelligence committee (JIC) was established to produce intelligence reports for the Joint Chiefs of Staff and the "higher authorities" of the United States.

SUPREME HEADQUARTERS ALLIED EXPEDITIONARY FORCE Office of Assistant Chief of Staff, G-2   November 1944 INTELLIGENCE REPORT NO. EW-Pa 128

SUBJECT: Plans of German industrialists to engage in underground activity after Germany's defeat; flow of capital to neutral countries.
SOURCE: Agent of French Deuxieme Bureau, recommendedvalero by Commandant Zindel. This agent is regarded as reliable and has worked for Quote from: *Larry Valeero U.S. Security Agency (Valero Report*

The **Valero Report** makes several interesting and pertinent points:
1. It quotes an October 1945 JIC report: "the USSR's <u>probable</u> course of action would be <u>rapidly increase size and capabilities of its air forces</u>."

2. "The release of the secret of atomic energy would only put the Soviets on an equal footing with the US and would possibly save them several years of research."

3. "JIC began to formulate rudimentary ideas about marriage of atomic weapons and other "weapons of mass destruction"--chemical and biological weapons and their means of delivery.

4. "There was no immediate Soviet threat to the continental United States"

5. "The JIC warned of the development of an intensive Soviet scientific research program designed to produce new weapons such as the atomic bomb ... these new developments in Soviet weaponry <u>could not be estimated with absolute precision</u>." (emphasis added)

6. "the Soviets would require approximately 15 years or more to build up the war industry needed to support large-scale offensive operations. ... "In a war with the Soviet Union we must envisage complete and total hostilities unrestricted in any way on the Soviet ...the United States had to be prepared for gas, bacteriological, and atomic warfare with USSR."

7. "It is not known if the JIC estimates, including JCS 1696, reached the President's desk. The estimates had a limited circulation.

8. "NSC 68 "argued that if US-Soviet antagonism continued, the West would succumb completely to the weight of international Communism. ...

As Secretary of State Acheson once stated, the purpose of NSC 68 was to "bludgeon the mass mind of 'top government' NSC 68 was an ideologically charged document, presumably designed to frighten the US leadership into making fundamental changes to national security policy.

9. Because JIC 397 had limited motivations, it probably was a more accurate reflection of the general mindset within the JIC and the larger JCS organization with regard to Soviet postwar military intentions and capabilities."

10. "The JIC was bureaucratically, after all, a military organization despite its nominal civilian membership. It was initially created to counter the encroachment of William Donovan into the Byzantine world of military intelligence. This was a fact that adherents of cenralized intelligence would not long forget."

Valero concludes the report: "The main problem facing the JIC was that it suffered from the same inter-service rivalries that plagued the larger US intelligence system and the US armed services as a whole during World War II and the early postwar period. The most notable bureaucratic conflict involved Army intelligence and the OSS. The Army would reject out of hand the contributions made by the Research and Analysis Branch of the OSS. Ludwell Lee Montague, while JIC Secretary, appreciated the analytic contributions of the OSS. In fact, Montague considered OSS estimates better founded than the assessments made by Army intelligence, which he criticized as being "derived from little more than...preconceptions."

Source: Memorandum for the Record, Intelligence Service, 1940-1950, 1 December 1969, HS/HC-401, RG 263, NACP. This document is an autobiographical account of Ludwell Lee Montague'sservice record during the 1940s. (emphasis added)

Aggravating the problems of the JIC system, civilian JIS members were rarely involved in areas clearly the domain of the Army and Navy intelligence services. Yet the military representatives of the JIS often considered themselves more than capable of making assessments on political and economic matters.

In addition, civilian members of the JIC system were not treated as equals with their military counterparts. Secrecy came into consideration. In some cases, the civilian members were excluded from deliberations on JIC estimates out of fear that military plans could be compromised. If political or economic considerations were needed, the military representatives would use their best judgment without inquiring into the civilian members' views.

Even worse for the JIC, the methods used for selecting the chiefs of the military intelligence services and the chairman of the JIS bore little relation to the qualifications needed for a competent intelligence professional, much less a leader of a joint intelligence organization. As Montague observed, "considerations of prestige, or the desire to find a place for tired naval officers between periods of sea duty, often seem to be the criteria for selection.

Despite its bureaucratic difficulties, the JIC was the centerpiece of the US intelligence effort during World War II. The JIC also played a crucial supporting role in the establishment of the US intelligence community, as we know it today.   Yet more intriguing are the JIC estimates of the USSR during the formative years of this century's great superpower conflict. These early estimates provide us with a tantalizing look at the Soviet threat from the unique standpoint of the JCS and its intelligence apparatus. The little-known story of the American JIC is an important chapter in US intelligence history dealing with the early years of the Cold War. (Valero Report, emphasis added)

Like the material on SAFEHAVEN, this section comes from the website and historical material of the CIA. It shows a military based and driven organization setting up Operation Paperclip. It was an organization whose main aim was to overcome the Soviets. It shows a group of military men who basically want a military desk job in their retirement. They had little sense of the economic and political consequences and causes of war. As Valero pointed out, there is little known about this group and their influence in shaping U.S. foreign policy. When there is no war, they create a "cold war". It is in this environment that OPERATION PAPERCLIP began and was carried out.

Few Americans have heard of Project Paperclip. Those who have, the majority do not know its true extent. The U.S. government has successfully concealed most facts about the project.

The government passed it off as a   short-term operation limited   to   an innocent Investigation of Germany's scientists after World War II. In reality, Project Paperclip, as documented by authors e.g. John Loftus in *The Belarus Secret*, was the largest/longest-running operation about Nazis in the history of the   United   States.   Its   effects   are   still   being   felt   today.

At the close of World War II, U.S. officials and the Allied countries discovered Germany had developed a technical superiority far beyond what they had imagined. In Nazi Germany, 20,000 scientists had revolutionized the weapons of war. Reports from Allied investigators described the Germans' "astonishing achievement" and "superb inventions." In order to learn about the new German technology and weaponry, Russia, France, Britain and the U.S began transporting German experts to their respective countries for interrogation.

The Cold War was beginning. U.S. officials were determined to use any means necessary to keep scientists responsible for Germany's scientific supremacy out of Russian hands.

At the same time, they aimed to acquire a technological lead against Russia. In the name of national interest, the U.S. began recruiting the Nazi scientists. In 1946, President Truman authorized Project Paperclip a program designed to bring selected German scientists to work for the U.S. in the Cold War.

Truman expressly forbade admitting anyone who had been "a member of the Nazi party and more than a nominal participant in its activities, or an active supporter of Nazism." The War Department's Joint Intelligence Objectives Agency (JIOA) was to conduct background investigations of scientists approved by the State Department.

Against Truman's orders, the JIOA, Army intelligence and the CIA actively concealed incriminating information about Germans they were hiring. Many of the 1,600 scientific and research specialists brought to the U.S. under Project Paperclip had been deeply involved in Nazi society during the war. U.S. officials were determined to recruit these men and to ignore their appalling pasts.

They sidestepped the problem of their Nazi backgrounds by "cleansing" and re-writing their information files to eliminate incriminating evidence. As a way of identifying the German scientists, American officials put an ordinary paperclip on their personnel files--thus the origin of the operation's name.

While official American policy after the war was to prosecute war criminals for atrocities committed under Adolf Hitler, many sectors of the U.S. government were actively concealing incriminating evidence in order to bring these very men into the U.S. Here are a few examples:

Early security evaluations of Wernher von Braun described him as "a serious potential security threat" a member of the SS and risen to the rank of major under Hitler. From 1937 to 1945, he was the technical director of the Peenemunde rocket research center in Germany, where the V-2 rocket was developed. von Braun was brought to the U.S. in 1948, his file was re-written.

"No derogatory information is available on the subject. He does not constitute a security threat to the United States." Von Braun worked on guided missiles for the U.S. Army and later became director of NASA's Marshall Space Flight Center In 1970. Later, he returned to Germany.

Kurt Blome, a high-ranking Nazi scientist, told U.S. interrogators in 1945 he had experimented with plague vaccines on concentration camp prisoners. He was tried in the Nuremberg War Trials but acquitted. The charge was extermination of sick prisoners and conducting experiments on humans. Two months after the trial he was interviewed at Camp David, Md., about his scientific expertise. His file now showed no record of his Nuremberg Trial. Blome was hired by the U.S. Army Chemical Corps to work on chemical and biological warfare.

Hermann Becker-Freysing was convicted at Nuremberg and sentenced to 20 years in prison for conducting experiments on Dachau concentration camp inmates by starving them and force-feeding them with chemically altered seawater. Before the trial he was being paid by the Army Air Force to write reports about his inhumane experiments.

George Richkey worked for the JIOA at Wright Field from 1946 until his arrest a year later for Nazi war crimes. During the war, he headed the slave labor factory Mittelwerk at the Dora concentration camps. Among other atrocities, there are reports that Richkey had numerous slave laborers hung from a crane to die slowly in public view. During his time in the United States, Richkey's job was to translate 42 boxes of Mittelwerk documents shipped from Normandy--the very documents a U.S. Army war crimes unit sought to use as evidence of Richkey's own crimes.

Defenders of Project Paperclip cite achievements such as the moon rockets and jet planes as positive products of postwar research in our country. But what Paperclip's defenders fail to mention is the shockingly inhumane psychochemical experimentation conducted on over 7,000 U.S. soldiers under the project. Edgewood Arsenal, near Baltimore, Md., is the most secret military base in the country. Paperclip scientists worked there between 1947 and 1966 conducting experiments on human beings. Initially, their main efforts were to test the poison gases that had been invented by the Nazis during the war. Soon, the testing turned to LSD and other mind-control agents. Nazi science reminiscent of concentration camp experimentation was used as the basis for research in the United States on humans.

MKULTRA is the name of the mind control experiments conducted on U.S. soldiers under Project Paperclip. Reviewing the experiments in the late 1950s, one CIA auditor wrote of them: "Precautions must be taken not only to protect operations from exposure to enemy forces but also to conceal these activities from the American public in general. The knowledge that the agency is engaging in unethical and illicit activities

Master Sergeant James Stanley, for one, remembers being locked in an isolated room with barred windows, padded walls and furniture bolted to the floor. A doctor instructed him to drink a glass of clear liquid containing LSD, telling him it was water. An hour later, Stanley's head filled with terrifying visions and he became violently ill.

In 1992, the highly respected physician Dr. D.C. Hammond lectured on hypnosis and satanic ritual abuse at the Conference on Abuse and Multiple Personality. He spoke of horrifying brainwashing methods being used in the same way all over the country, he notes its beginning:

Here's where it appears to have come from. At the end of World War II, before it even ended, Allen Dulles and people from our Intelligence Community were already in Switzerland making contact to get out Nazi scientists. As World War II ends, they not only get out rocket scientists, but they also get out some Nazi doctors who have been doing mind-control research in the camps. They brought them to the United States.

Men responsible for atrocities under Hitler were recruited to fight the Cold War. This resulted in serious breaches of U.S. security and extremely inhumane treatment of American soldiers, similar to concentration camp prisoners.

On the security level, as **Linda Hunt** writes in <u>**Secret Agenda:**</u>

In direct defiance of President Truman's policy, the Paperclip masterminds brazenly had the German scientists' records changed to erase evidence of war crimes and ardent Nazism and secure permanent immigration status for them in the U.S. Ostensibly that was done in the interest of national security. Once here, however, the scientists were given access to classified information that revealed the inner-most workings of our defense system. As a result, it was not long before the very people brought here to ensure our security become a security risk. Eventually some of the scientists took advantage of security lapses and left the country with classified material. German specialist Heinz Gartmann, for example, left Wright Field air base with turbojet rocket engine blueprints in his hand luggage. Full extent of the damage from incidents like that is still unknown.

Even worse, on a moral level, Nazis went unpunished and federal law was violated. Worst of all, as Linda Hunt has documented, Nazi attitudes toward research on human subjects were imported and adopted by various U.S. officials. "The Machiavellian attitude behind these operations was born when a World War II ally became a new enemy and the world axis shifted [but] no matter how necessary intelligence activities may be, they cannot be allowed to operate unchecked in secrecy and darkness shielded from the democratic process of accountability. Otherwise, we become our own worst enemy."
Cf.. Linda Hunt   <u>Secret Agenda</u>

WHAT HAPPENED TO LEADERS OF IG Farben?

Some were convicted of war crimes but were released within a short time. Several ended up heads of their corporations.

Fritz ter Meer (1884-1967) was a Member of the IG Farben executive committee 1926-1945, member of the working committee and technical committee, director of section II. In 1943 he was plenipotentiary for Italy of the Reich Minister for armaments and war production, military economist chief industrialist responsible for Auschwitz.

In 1948 he was found guilty of "plundering" and "enslavement" and condemned to seven years detention. He was released in 1952. In 1955 board member of Bayer, 1956-1964 chairman of the board of Bayer he be became chairman of the board or deputy chairman of the board of 22 banks and the bank association West Germany AG and the United Industrial enterprises AG (VIAG)

Otto Ambros was a member of the IG Farben executive committee 1938-1945, member of the chemical committee and chairman of commission K (agents), special advisors of Krauchs F department for the four-year plan, director of the special committee C (chemical agents), the main committee for powders and explosives in the office for arms, military industrial leader. He was responsible for running IG Auschwitz as operations manager and synthetic fuel production. In 1948 he was found guilty of "enslavement" and condemned to eight years detention He was released in 1952. Starting in 1954 he became chairman, deputy chairmen and member of the boards of: several corporations.

Hermann Schmitz was a member of the IG Farben executive committee 1926-1935, chairman of the board 1935-1945 and "head of finances" to IG, head of military economics, member of the Nazi party (NSDAP) 1948 found guilty of "plundering" condemned to four years in prison released 1950. In 1952 board member of the German bank Berlin West 1956 honorary chairman of the board of Rheinish steel plants.

Fritz Gajewski was a member of the IG Farben executive committee 1931-1945, head of section III (point of contact to Dynamite Nobel).

Carl Krauch was a member of the IG Farben executive committee 1926-1940, chairman of the board 1940-1945, director of coordination center, director of the Reich office for economics, plenipotentiary for special questions on chemical production, military industrial leader.

In 1948 he was found guilty of "enslavemnt" and condemned to six years in prison. He was released in 1950. By 1955 he was a board member of Huels GmbH.

Carl Wurster was a member of the IG Farben executive committee 1938-1945, director of BG upper Rhine, board member of DEGESCH, head of military economics and member of the military economic advisory council of the Reich chamber of economics. At Nuremberg, he was "not guiltily" of all charges. In 1952 he was chairman of the board of the "new" BASF, and 2 other corporations and member of the board for 6 other corporations.

http://www4.dr-rath-oundation.org/PHARMACEUTICAL_BUSINESS/history_of_the_pharmaceutical_industry.htm

There were 8 members of the IG Farben executive committee. All were charged with crimes at Nuremberg in 1948. 6 were found guilty. 4 were released by 1950., the other 2 in 1951. All quickly made a member of the board of at least 1 became chairman of the board of at least one corporation. This group provided the chairman of the board for the 3 major corporations into which IG Farben was split. 1 became chairman of the board of the group which oversaw the dissolution of IG Farben. They were members of the board of 4 different banks. In those cases one person became the chairman of the board. Was IG Farben really dissolved?

BASF

Why are we looking at IG Farben? Ithas not existed for over 50 years? Its history goes back almost 200 years and the corporations it has formed still exist today. Why is this important today? The answer can be seen at the end of the prolog Diarmuid Jeffrey's book Hell's Cartel and the Making of Hitler's War Machine. ... it contains warning about the dangers inherent in any close relationship between business and the state and what can go wrong when political objectives and the pursuit of profit become dangerously intertwined. op. cit. p. 10 end of prologue

A calendar may be helpful in looking at the history of Bayer

1820's dyes discovered and become valuable product

1861 Bayer founded representative to USA appointed

1863 Hoescht founded

1865 BASF (Badische Anilin und Soda Fabrik) was founded.

1867 Agfa founded (Bayer Hoescht BASF Agfa became IG Farben

1872 German Reich founded, prior to Reich 30 independent states

1876 major synthetic dye companies Britain 5 France, 17 Germany

1880 Hoescht moved into Pharmaceutical market

1890 German tariff fees, companies begin trading in other nations

1903 Carl Duisberg of Bayer visits Standard Oil (USA) gets idea of a cartel

1904 Duisberg proposes similar cartel for German dye companies

1904 loose confederation of Bayer BASF and Agfa formed

1914 World War 1 begins

1914 British blockade prevents German exports and imports

1915 poison made by German cartel companies and is used in war

1916 small version of IG Farben formed

1917 USA enters World War 1

1919 World War 1 ends Versailles treaty puts economic barriers on

1924 German sanctions more foreign competition for German industry

1925 IG Farben founded

1926 Farben and U.S companies meet to set up international cartel

1929 Great depression   USA, Germany hard hit

The four major corporations in IG Farben: BASF, Bayer, Hoechst, and Agfa were founded in the 1860's. By 1875 the industry spread to Britain and France, soon to the USA. In 1904 an official of Bayer visited Standard Oil USA. He was impressed by the cartel Standard had formed. He wanted to form a similar union with German chemical corporations.

In a short time he was able to form a loose confederation of Bayer, BASF, and Hoechst. This was the beginning of what was later to become IG Farben. Even though the individual corporations had proxy companies in the USA, the war posed major difficulties in transporting needed supplies and finished products between nations. This experience convinced many corporate officials that they needed to work together. Eventually that led to the formation of IG Farben. It was formed in 1925. By 1926 officials of Farben met with U.S. companies hoping to set up an international cartel. Although no cartel was formed, trade links were formed. Those links were so strong a world war could not break them.

A calendar of the war years:

1914 World War One began U.S. trade with Germany $170 million ($4.15 BILLION in today's currency) German corporations in US created as proxy corporations to mask German origin   1915 Germans used gas as a military weapon and Bayer created gas
itish retaliate by creating and using gas chemical Companies like BASF Bayer depended on government contracts shortage of materials and /embargoes cause chemical companies to work together
1916 informal cooperation began among chemical companies and between chemical and munitions factories a large military meant fewer workers to create ammunition this led to hiring of women and children, ultimately to slave labor   1917 USA enters war Russian revolution and downfall of government
1918 German holdings in USA $950 million ($23.2 BILLION in today's currency) war ends
1919   Treaty   of   Versailles: its   regulations   devastate   Germany as a result of Treaty Sterling Chemical (US corporation) takes over Bayer
1921 chemical plant at Oppau devastated by explosion over 600 persons killed, 200,000 injured, causes never determined

At the end of the war (WW1) most of Europe was on the verge of bankruptcy. Germany was especially hard hit. This helped spark a worldwide depression. Many reasons have been given for that depression: the huge debt for military expenses, layoffs when military supplies were no longer needed, huge borrowing to pay debts, and excessive printing of money.

In 1924 prior to the depression a plan for the rehabilitation of Germany was proposed by Charles Dawes. The plan called for the removal of Allied troops from Germany who was to begin paying reparations payments at once. The German Central Bank was to be reorganized under Allied supervision. The USA was to loan Germany 800 million Marks.

The plan seemed to be a boon to Germany. However, it made Germany dependent on foreign loans and foreign imports. Germany refused to make the payments and the Young plan was introduced to succeed it. This plan reduced Germans payments to 20% and set up the Bank for International Settlements (BIS) to succeed it. For more on BIS cf. ch 1 above and ch 6 Why We Are Always Broke

In the midst of this economic confusion, the major chemical plants of Germany decided to merge into IG Farben. It was a merger of BASF, Bayer, Hoechst, Agfa and several smaller corporations. In the midst of that same economic confusion, Hitler was able to gain enough support to take political control of Germany. It is not surprising that these two German forces would come together. IG Farben could not exist without government support. Hitler could not succeed without financial support, which IG Farben helped supply. Once Hitler decided to extend beyond Germany, war was inevitable. IG Farben supplied the materials he needed to wage war.

Before IG Farben was formed, an official of Bayer (eventually a member of IG Farben) made a trip to New York. He was fascinated by the cartel that Standard Oil had created. He wondered why the chemical and pharmaceutical companies of Germany could not form a similar cartel. He proposed the idea to other corporations. He managed to form a loosely knit coalition but nothing like he would have hoped for. It was not until the troubles after World War 1 that he was able to get the support that resulted in IG Farben.

With the formation of IG Farben, BASF no longer acted as an independent corporation. To trace BASF history from 1925 to the end of World War 2, we need to look at IG Farben. Within a short time Standard Oil and IG Farben invested in a joint research plan to create synthetic fuels. Ultimately they built a plant in Louisiana to create synthetic fuel.

There were two problems that hampered this project. A unit of Farben, BASF, owned the patent for the project. This problem was solved by allowing Standard Oil to use the process anywhere in the world except Germany.

In return IG Farben would buy 2% of Standard Oil stock. The second problem was not as easily solved. New oil fields were discovered in the Mid-East. The production of synthetic fuels became more expensive than taking the oil from the newly discovered fields. Still a corporation was formed, Joint American Study Company (JASCO). I have been unable to find any reference to any accomplishments of JASCO.

Still, a coalition between Farben and U.S. corporations was definitely established. Standard Oil had many links with U.S. banks. Now IG Farben enjoyed those same links. By now a violent revolution was taking place in Germany. Economic disorders in Germany led to Hitler seizing power and the rise of the Nazis. As he Nazis grew stronger, IG Farben had two choices: either ignore the political changes or join with them and seek a way to profit from that alliance. IG Farben chose the latter course.

As word of Hitler's atrocities spread around the world, Germany became the subject of many embargoes. These coalesced with Hitler's attitude of forming a super race. The discovery of new oil fields made synthetic fuels less desirable elsewhere. Germany was seeking to create its own source of fuel. IG Farben had the technology to create synthetic fuels. That was one possible way IG Farben could profit from the rise of Nazism.

Creation of its own synthetic fuels had side effects. IG Farben signed a contract with Hitler. The Government will finance IG Farben's manufacture of synthetic oil. Germany was now able to create fuels which would propel planes. These planes were able to fly faster and longer than anything previously known. The super planes fit well with Hitler's idea of conquering the world. A deeper union between Hitler and IG Farben was created. Farben's philosophy was more clearly defined: We will support any movement, any party which helps us make money.

If you look for direct connections between Hitler and U.S. banks they are hard to find. They were well concealed. Once you break down the camouflage you see connections. For example, the banking house of Brown Brothers-Harriman and its various fronts funded Hitler. US citizens, some of them very prominent citizens, began funding Hitler as early as 1923. They even set up Union Banking Corporation to handle funds from the Thyssen family which owned the German Steel Trust. Thyssen and his work are not as well-known as IG Farben but they also created war material for the Nazis and used the same methods including slave labor. In addition to its contract with Standard Oil, IG Farben created U S based corporations to hide money and distribute products.

The assured source of money and corporations willing to create the products was all Hitler needed to begin a more aggressive campaign and begin extending his ambitions beyond the boundaries of Germany. Hitler's advisors devised a four year plan preparing for war. In the first six months 100 million Reichmarks were allotted to prepare for war. 90% of that money was to go to the chemical industry, 70% to IG Farben.

As the pace of the war picked up, IG Farben saw more and more offices, factories, and subsidiaries working directly for the Government. They were less able to oversee everything that happened in IG Farben. This has led some to say that IG Farben was not to blame for the Holocaust. In fact, IG Farben could not have survived without Hitler to fund and support them financially. Hitler also could not have survived, certainly not done the damage he did, without IG Farben. They formed a partnership. Both share the blame. Both reaped the benefits.

As Hitler annexed new territories, IG Farben took over the chemical plants in the annexed territories. IG Farben sent its spies before areas were invaded. IG Farben was looking for new chemical plants to take over. They shared spy information with Hitler. While people in Poland were still fleeing from Hitler's invasion, IG Farben was seizing chemical plants. Before World War Two began a British company, ICI, signed an agreement with IG Farben, which established production quotas for nitrogen, the main ingredient in fertilizer. In 1935 the companies agreed that IG Farben would sell nitrogen in all of Europe, except Spain and Portugal, as well as South and Central America, while ICI would control the markets in the United Kingdom, Spain, Portugal, Indonesia, and the Canary Islands. And they agreed to share the Asian market.

http://www.referenceforbusiness.com/history2/19/Imperial-Chemical-Industries-PLC.html#ixzz3dB2aaZsX

Apparently the IG Farben/ICI (Imperial Chemical Industries) agreement had little advantage to ICI. IG Farben through BASF continued to produce nitrogen. ICI signed an agreement with the U.S. Government to work together on the development of a nuclear bomb. Eventually the British left that process to the USA. Still, in 1944 the British-American group sent a person to Germany to find the blueprint and other material on the bomb possessed by the IG Farben cartel.

In June, 1941 Hitler began Operation Barbarossa. The project involved the invasion of Russia. On the invasion of Russia, I found no collaboration between IG Farben and Hitler at least no direct collaboration.

IG Farben benefitted from the operation. Heinrich Himmler, commander of SS saw Auschwitz as a place where SS prisoners would work as slave laborers and the SS would profit by selling coal, gravel and human labor for the profit of the SS. Himmler ordered Auschwitz capacity for prisoners to be tripled. This is not the only example of Auschwitz and IG Farben being used for the benefit of the SS or the Nazi Party. That raises a question was IG Farben and its various arms owned by IG Farben or by Hitler and the Nazi Party? A partial answer can be found in Wikipedia. Under the title IG Farben is the following quote: "Contrary to other industries, the founders and their families had little influence on the top-level decision-making of the leading German chemical firms, which was in the hands of professional salaried managers. This unique situation, the economic historian Alfred Chandler called the German dye companies "the world's first truly managerial industrial enterprises".

en.wikipedia.org/wiki/IG_Farnen.wikipedia.org/wiki/IG_Farnen.wikipedia.org/wiki/IG_Farnen.wikipedia.org/wiki/IG_Farn

Ctaken from Chandler, Alfred DuPont (2004), Scale and Scope: The Dynamics ofIndustria C Capitalism, Cambridge, MA: Belknap Press of Harvard University Press, _

There is no reason to suspect any change in the governing of the new cartel, especially since many of the top leaders also led the individual corporations which made up IG Faren. The question is who were the managers of IG Farben? Hemann Schmitz was chairman of the board.

He was also a member of the Nazi party and was instrumental in establishing the policy of IG Farben. Carl Krauch was head of research and development for the "Four Year Plan" by which Germany was to invade other nations. In that position he was able to direct funds to IG Farben. Fritz der Meer had full powers in Italy to represent the Reich minister for armaments and war production. Otto Ambros was a special advisor to one of the departments for the four year plan. Carl Wurster served as an ambassador for the Reich Office of Economic Expansion. All power for IG Farben rested in its managers. Several were double agents. They worked for the Reich and for IG Farben.

A US Military Intelligence report EW-Pa 128 Enclosure No. 1 to dispatch No. 19,489 of Nov. 27, 1944, from the Embassy at London England stated that a meeting of the principal German industrialists with interests in France was held on August 10, 1944, in the Hotel Rotes Haus in Strasbourg, France with representatives of S.S. leaders and the major industries of Germany and Poland present

Ministry of Armament, Paris.

At the meeting Dr. Scheid stated that all industrial material in France was to be evacuated to Germany immediately. The battle of France was lost for Germany. Now the German industry must realize that the war cannot be won and we must take steps in preparation for a post-war commercial campaign. Each industrialist must make contacts and alliances with foreign firms the ground has to be laid on the financial level for borrowing considerable sums from foreign countries after the war. As examples, Dr. Scheid cited the fact that patents for stainless steel belonged to the Chemical Foundation, Inc., New York, the Krupp company of Germany jointly and that the U.S. Steel Corporation, Carnegie Illinois, American Steel and Wire, and National Tube, etc. were thereby under an obligation to work with the Krupp concern. He also cited the Zeiss Company, Leisa Company and the Hamburg-American Line as firms which had been especially effective in protecting German interests abroad and gave their New York address to the industrialists.

Following this meeting a smaller one was held presided over by Dr. Bosse of the German Armaments Ministry and attended only by representatives of Hecho, Krupp and Rochling. At this second meeting it was stated that the Nazi Party had informed the industrialists that the war was practically lost but that it would continue until a guarantee of the unity of Germany could be obtained. German industrialists must, through their exports increase the strength of Germany. They must also prepare themselves to finance the Nazi Party which would be forced to go underground as Maquis (in Gebirgaverteidigungastellenehen).

Existing financial reserves in foreign countries must be placed at the disposal of the Party so that a strong German Empire can be created after the defeat. It is required that the large factories in Germany create small technical offices or research bureaus. The prohibition against the export of capital which was rigorously enforced until now has been completely withdrawn and replaced by a new Nazi policy whereby industrialists with government assistance will export as much of their capital as possible. The Nazi party stands behind the industrialists and urges them to save themselves by getting funds outside Germany and advance the party's plans for its post-war operation.

The freedom given the industrialists further cements their relations with the Party by giving them a measure of protection. The German industrialists are not only buying agricultural property in Germany but are placing their funds abroad, particularly in neutral countries. Two main banks through which this export of capital operates are the Basler Handelsbank and the Schweizerische Kreditanstalt of Zurich. Also there are a number of agencies in Switzerland which for a 5 percent commission buy property in Switzerland, using a Swiss cloak.

The Nazi Party recognizes certain best known leaders will be condemned. However, in cooperation with the industrialists it is arranging to place less conspicuous but important members in positions with various German factories as technical experts or members of its research and designing offices. From the A.C. f S., G-2. WALTER K. SCHWINN G-2, Economic Section Prepared by MEVIN M. FAGEN Distribution: Same as EW-Pa 1, U.S. Political Adviser, SHAEF British Political Adviser, SHAEF

Schweizerische Kreditanstalt of Zurich became Credit Suisse and eventually admitted it received money, gold, and precious items from the Nazis and from Jews. It admitted the bank still has some of those items. One of the employees of Credit Suisse, Christoph Meili, testified at a US Senate hearing:

One of the things that I have learned in these last few months is that there are certain powers in Switzerland that do not want to see the Swiss Banks and our government exposed for what they did during the Holocaust and that they will do anything - including destroying documents restricting and controlling Police investigations, hiding burying evidence and lying publicly.

The energy deal between Russia and Germany effectively shows that political tension between Russia and the West over Ukraine and Crimea has little to do with real business. The leaders of the US and the EU are gathering on Monday in Brussels to discuss sanctions against Russia. They are largely expected to be limited to visa bans and an asset freeze for some of Russia's leading officials, not corporate assets

In 2012, over 6,000 German companies were registered in Russia. These firms had a combined turnover of €40bn and employed around 270,000 people. In Germany, 350,000 jobs are estimated to depend on business with Russia.

German firms have invested in excess of €22bn in Russia with Siemens, Volkswagen, BASF, Metro and Henkel among the leading players. In 2013, 132,400 German cars were sold in Russia and German mechanical engineering companies achieved €9.5bn in turnover from their Russian trade. The percentage of turnover dependent on Russian trade has been increasing for many leading German firms e.g. BASF 14%, Metro 8%, Adidas 7% The Institute of International and European Affairs understands German-Russian Trade affairs.

http://www.iiea.com/blogosphere/understanding-german-russian-tradehttp:

BASF is a member of MRDI which is a member of Global SOF "a sales and engineering firm which focus on military and government market." SOF "brings together military, government, industry, and intellectual leaders from around the world for the purpose of advancing the capability and efficacy of SOF." All of its material speaks about promoting SOF, not furthering peace or other humanitarian work. Sounds much like IG Farben. quotes taken from website SOF Foundation website

World War Two was the first time chemical weapons were used on such a large scale. As the war was ending Germany, England, and the United States were working toward the creation of a nuclear bomb which could destroy thousands of people in a very short time. That war ended only when the USA dropped bombs on Hiroshima and Nagasaki. Although it ended that war, more importantly, it set a definite pattern. Future wars would be chemical wars. BASF and other component parts of IG Farben would play critical roles in such wars. IG Farben was "dissolved" at the end of the war. The corporations which made up IG Farben were split into separate corporations. IG Farben still existed as a "trust". I use that word in a sarcastic way. Its money was to be used to pay off the damages done by its activities. It was dissolved when many survivors or relatives of survivors of the Holocaust began demanding reparation for the Holocaust. IG Farben was completely dissolved a few years ago. No money in its "trust" fund was used as reparation to the victims of IG Farben. The money was used to pay off any debts still owed by IG Farben to banks. BASF and other parts of IG Farben who still exist were not held responsible. The skeletons of IG Farben continued their destructive work.

When IG Farben was "dissolved" it was split into three major corporations who made up IG Farben: Hoescht, BASF, and Bayer. Hoescht. seems to have played a predominant role in the "formation" of IG Farben corporations, BASF played a very prominent role in IG Farben which was fourth largest overall industrial concern, after Standard Oil of New Jersey, General Motors and U.S. Steel. Today according to Fortune 500, Exxon-Mobil, one of Standard Oil's successor is the second largest company, Chevron, another of Standard's successors is number 12. General Motors is the sixth largest.

If "IG Farben in liquidation" did not receive government funding "it would be obliged to dram on the assets of its successor companies". IG Farben when economically threatened recognized its connections. with successor corporations. BUT successor corporations do not wish to recognize the same relationship in regard to victims. Wurster, Haberland, & Winnacker were heads of the 3 successor corporations. They continued meet after the split.   cf. Inside IG Farben p 364-365

Actually profit increases ranged up to 2,431 percent for whole industries and up to 11,743 percent for individual concerns. Following are Office of Price Administration figures for percentage increases of 1944 profits over 1936-39 averages, by industries (Congressional Record, January 22, 1946):

Motor vehicle parts 896%	Iron, steel and by-products 252%
Lumber and timber by-products 1,064 %	Electrical machinery 434%
Communications equipment 521%	Industrial electrical equipment 99%
Other electrical products 772%	Non-electrical machinery 360%
Engines and turbines 2,431%	Transportation equipment 658%
Aircraft and parts 1,686%	Railroad equipment 318%
Food and kindred products 150%	Meat products 271%
Apparel 280%	Textile mill products 522%
petroleum and coal products 159 %	Rubber products 698%
Bituminous and other soft coal 1,148%	

Although IG Farben was shut down in 1945, reorganization did not achieve any real success until December 1951. Then within a few weeks three individual corporations were formed (BASF Bayer Hoescht). There were several reasons it took so long. Germany had been divided into four different segments. Each segment was controlled by a different nation (Britain, France, USA. USSR). Each of those nations had a different idea how Germany should be rebuilt. Several of the top officials of IG Farben were on trial.

There were internal struggles about who would run the individual corporations. There were struggles about who was at fault, which was fit to run the new corporations.   Although 18 of the defendants in the Nuremberg Trial received prison sentences, all were released by the early 1950's. They played an important role in the formation of the final corporations. Several resumed former positions.

There were 22 different plants under IG Farben's control. Those plants were scattered in each one of the four divided segments of Germany. The military personnel who headed each section were battle weary and wanted to return home. They were not interested in how Germany was divided or what happened to the remnants of IG Farben and so its reorganization was pretty much left to the German people. Like IG Farben, BASF added a German subtitle to its name BASF KTIENGESELLSCHAFT. The subtitle means corporation with shares of stock.   In this way BASF differed from IG Farben.   In many ways they were similar. That is not surprising since BASF is a daughter company of IG Farben. BASF is 75% owned by investment owners. Black Rock owns more than 5%. German investors own 36% of BASF, US investor 17% and British 11%. I could not discern if among them there were any groups which owned shares in BASF under different names. Like IG Farben, BASF split into different areas. That did not stop it from doing illegal things in each.

Like IG Farben, BASF had formed a cartel which the Depart of Justice called a "conspiracy" and they were fined $1.1 BILLION for fixing the price of vitamins.

Any connection between remnant countries of IG Farben and the deadly gasses produced today has been carefully camouflaged. However sarin a deadly element in chemical weapons was created by BASF and Bayer. BASF seems to take a different approach today. It is manufacturing elements used to overcome the effects of deadly chemical weapons. So IG Farben's children are still making money off chemical disasters. These are supported by the government, which caused the disaster in the first place. The children of IG Farben and other chemical manufacturers are also dumping harmful and pollutant elements into our air and our waters. Some things never change.

In 2002 BASF appointed a new chairman. He identified five factors he wished to pursue as chairman. The first was to develop the petrochemical resources now available because of the US war with Iraq. The second was to work with government and international groups to soften economic impact from harsher environmental regulations. The third was to join together various chemical corporations in order to create a stronger more diversified corporation. The fourth was to expand BASF throughout the world. One of the places he highlights is China. It is no coincidence that two of the top three corporations in the world, according to Forbes, are Chinese petroleum corporations. The final goal is to attract top chemists to BASF. That plan of the new chairman sounds like the plan of IG Farben.

Like IG Farben, BASF was to employ intelligence agents (spies?) to help create a unified, central policy for BASF. In our day it is not just automobile mauufacturerrs, there is now an international group, Global Intelligence Alliance, training corporations in the tool of IG Farben.

> Global Intelligence Alliance (GIA) is a strategic market intelligence and advisory group. GIA was formed in 1995 when a team of market intelligence specialists, management consultants, industry analysts and technology experts came together to build a powerful suite of customized solutions ranging from outsourced market monitoring services and software, to strategic analysis and advisory.

> Today, we are the preferred partner for organizations seeking to understand, compete and grow in international markets. Our industry expertise and coverage of over 100 countries enables our customers to make better informed decisions worldwide.

When we look at IG Farben and the corporations it has spawned, there is a major unanswered question. How can we have national security when the international cartels IG Farben spawned (some of which still exist) promote international insecurity? Some things have changed since IG Farben has been split. Despite the changes some things remain the same. Like IG Farben, Standard Oil has been split up.

Two of the companies into which it has been split Exxon-Mobil and Chevron are listed in Fortune 500 among the top 12 largest corporations in the world, now 2 other oil companies from China rank above either Exxon Mobil (#4) or Chevron (#12).

Where do the remnant companies of IG Farben rank? Bayer is #57. BASF is #75. Hoescht has become Sanifi which ranks #238. The current Fortune 500 reflects a similar yet slightly different world (at least business world) than IG Farben's world. Standard Oil, General Motors, and Ford were predominant corporations in the days of IG Farben. Today, 9 of the 12 largest corporations in the world produce oil and gas or manufacture automobiles. General Motors #21 and Ford #26 are smaller than Volkswagen (Germany) #8 and Toyota (Japan) #9. #17 Gazpron is a Russian oi company. It is 50% owned by Wintershall a 100% subsidiary of BASF.. While the USA has worked so hard to maintain military superiority, it is becoming weaker economically.

Meanwhile, BASF was expanding. In 1954 BASF established Consolidated Dyestuffs & Chemicals in Canada to act as the Canadian agent for BASF and in 1961 it became BASF Canada. In 1958 Dow Chemical Company and BASF jointly established Dow Badische Chemical Company. Dow left that joint venture 20 years later. In 1959 BASF bought Wyandotte Chemicals Corporation.

With its purchases BASF becomes the world leader in supplying polyurethane. In 1985 BASF buys Celanese Corporation, Inmont, and American Enka. In 1995 BASF moves into Mexico to take advantage of the NAFTA treaty. In 1998 BASF and FINA begin constructing the world's largest naphta seam cracker. In 2001 it begins producing propylene and ethylene. BASF acquires the Engelhard Corporation in 2006, Ciba in 2009 and Cognis in 2010.

These figures come from the BASF website.
http://www.basf.ca/group/corporate/ca/en/about-basf/worldwide/north-america/Canada/about-basf/history/index

BASF is 75% owned by investment owners. Black Rock owns more than 5%. German investors own 36% of BASF, US investors 17% and British 11%. I could not discern if among them there were any groups which owned shares in BASF under different names. Any connection between remnant countries of IG Farben and the deadly gasses produced today has been carefully camouflaged.

However, sarin a deadly element in chemical weapons was created by BASF and Bayer. BASF seems to take a different approach today. It is manufacturing elements used to overcome the effects of deadly chemical weapons. So IG Farben's children are still making money off of chemical disasters. These are supported by the government. A union of Government and BASF caused the disaster in the first place. The children of IG Farben and other chemical manufacturers are also dumping harmful and pollutant elements into our air and our waters. Some things never change!

In 2002 BASF appointed a new chairman. He identified five factors that he wished to pursue as chairman. The first was to develop the petrochemical resources now available because of the US war with Iraq. The second was to work with government and international groups to soften economic impact on harsher environmental regulations.

The third was to join together various chemical corporations in order to create a stronger more diversified corporation. The fourth was to expand BASF throughout the world. One of the places he highlights is China. It is no coincidence that two of the top three corporations in the world, according to Forbes, are Chinese petroleum corporations. The final goal is to attract top chemists to BASF. The new chairman's plan sounds very much like IG Farben in the 1940's!

Like IG Farben, BASF employed intelligence agents (spies?) to help create a unified, central policy for BASF. In our day it is not just IG Farben, Standard Oil, and a few automobile manufacturers, there is now an international group, Global Intelligence Alliance, training corporations in the tools of IG Farben.

Global Intelligence Alliance (GIA) is a strategic market intelligence and advisory group. GIA was formed in 1995 when a team of market intelligence specialists, management consultants, industry analysts and technology experts came together to build a powerful suite of customized solutions ranging from outsourced market monitoring services and software, to strategic analysis and advisory.

Today, we are the preferred partner for organizations seeking to understand, compete and grow in international markets. Our industry expertise and coverage of over 100 countries enables our customers to make better informed decisions worldwide.

When we look at IG Farben and the corporations it has spawned, there is a major unanswered question. How can we have national security when the international cartels IG Farben spawned (and which still exist) promote international insecurity?

BAYER

Fritz ter Meer was Chairman of the Supervisory Board of BAYER. He was on trial in Nuremberg. During his interrogation he said that the slave laborers in Auschwitz had 'not been made to suffer particularly badly as the individual laboratories, research was carried out into chemical war gases. The inventor of SARIN and TABUN, Dr. Gerhard Schrader, was head of the BAYER pesticides department after WW II. During the Vietnam War, BAYER was involved in the development of AGENT ORANGE. Production was carried out at the firm MOBAY, founded jointly by BAYER and MONSANTO". Excerpted from: "Press Release, March 21, 2013, Coalition against Bayer Dangers, 150th anniversary / Countermotions to shareholder meeting: BAYER: Company History Whitewashed" (Emphasis added; this and more:

Bayer claims it is no longer a legal entity related to IG Farben, and yet: BAYER honors war criminal Fritz ter Meer. Why, in November 2006, did the modern Bayer Corporation place a wreath from the "Bayer Board of Trustees and Supervisory Board" at the grave site of convicted Nuremberg war criminal Fritz ter Meer? Why does the post-1952 Bayer Corporation currently administer a scholarship fund named for this same individual?" "PRESS RELEASE, November 14, 2006, Coalition against Bayer Dangers, See more here: http://www.cbgnetwork.org/1695.html

Fritz ter Meer (July 4, 1884 – October 27, 1967) was a German chemist and Nazi war criminal. From 1925 to 1945 Fritz ter Meer was on the board of IG Farben AG. He was involved in the planning of Monowitz concentration camp, a satellite camp of KZ Auschwitz. He was sentenced to seven years in prison at Nuremberg Trials in 1948. He was released in 1951 and he became supervisory board chairman (Aufsichtsratsvorsitzender) of Bayer AG. .... He was released early in the summer of 1950 because of 'good behavior' in prison for war criminals from the prison in Landsberg and was given the removal of the restrictive clause of the Allied War Crimes Act No. 35 in 1956 and became Chairman of Bayer AG. In subsequent years, he also took on board positions at a number of other companies, including, several banks. His achievements in the reconstruction of the chemical industry in Germany are considered significant."

For almost three decades after the Second World War, BASF, Bayer and Hoechst (now Aventis) each filled its highest position, chairman of the board, with former members of the Nazi, NSDAP. Curt Hansen, chairman of the board of Bayer until the late 70's, was co-organizer of the conquest of Europe in the department of acquisition of raw materials."

Under this leadership the IG Farben daughters, BASF, Bayer, and Hoechst, continued to support politicians representing their interests. IG FARBEN was closely involved in the war of conquest of the Third Reich. The company followed the armed forces into the conquered countries of Europe and took over considerable parts of the chemical industry there within a few weeks. It also took over coal mines and oil production. The later Chairman of the BAYER Board of Management, Kurt Hansen, played a leading role in these robberies.

In the Nuremberg Trial IG FARBEN faced a trial of its own. One section, for example, states the following: 'It is undisputed that criminal experiments were undertaken by SS physicians on concentration camp prisoners. These experiments served the express purpose of testing the products of IG FARBEN." The managers condemned at Nuremberg were able to continue their careers unhindered after sitting out their sentences. Fritz ter Meer, for example, became Chairman of the Supervisory Board of BAYER. During his interrogation in Nuremberg, he said that the slave laborers in Auschwitz had 'not been made to suffer particularly badly as they were to have been killed anyway."

In BAYER laboratories, research was carried out into chemical war gases. The inventor of SARIN and TABUN, Dr. Gerhard Schrader, became head of the BAYER pesticides department after WW II. During the Vietnam war, BAYER was involved in the development of AGENT ORANGE. Production was carried out at the firm MOBAY, founded jointly by BAYER and MONSANTO". Excerpted from: "Press Release, March 21, 2013, Coalition against Bayer Dangers, 150th anniversary / Countermotions to shareholder meeting: BAYER: Company History Whitewashed" (Emphasis added; this and more: [Bayer claims it is no longer a legal entity related to IG Farben, and yet we read "PRESS RELEASE, November 14, 2006, Coalition against Bayer Dangers, We Read: BAYER honors war criminal Fritz ter Meer- http://www.cbgnetwork.org/1695.html

Bayer is implicated in the development of chemical weapons. During WW1 Bayer was involved in the development and manufacture of a range of poisonous gasses used in the trenches, including chlorine gas and mustard gas. As part of IG Farben, Bayer was also involved in the development of the next generation of chemical warfare agents, toxic organophosphate compounds. Tabun was first examined for use as an insecticide in late 1936 in a program under the direction of Dr. Gerhard Schrader at the Bayer facility at Elberfeld/Wuppertal. An accidental exposure of Dr. Schrader and a laboratory assistant to Tabun vapors made it quite clear that this compound had potential military applications. Tabun was mass produced by IG Farben during WWII although it was never used as a weapon.

Schrader was also responsible for the discovery of related, but more toxic, nerve agents including Sarin and Soman.[213] Whilst working on chemical weapons Schrader discovered the chemical compound E 605, the principle ingredient in the pesticide parathion. After the post-war dissolution of IG Farben, Schrader continued to develop pesticides for Bayer. After World War II, Bayer and other companies began to introduce a large number of organophosphorus compounds, including parathion, into the marketplace for insect control. The difficulty with organophosphates (OPs) is that they are neurotoxic due to their effects on acetycholinesterase, and unfortunately this enzyme occurs in humans as well as in insects.

The links between chemicals developed as 'pesticides' with chemicals suitable for weapons has continued at Bayer. In 1989 it was revealed that Bayer hold a patent for a compound chemically identical to the VX gas used by the US military. The compound was discovered by Gerhard Schrader, and was patented in Germany in 1957 and in the US in 1961. Bayer claims that the compound was developed as a potential pesticide and that the US military application of the compound has nothing to do with them.

Bayer, IG Farben and World War II: Slave Labor and Deadly Gas

Bayer was an original member of the IG Farben group. During WWII, IG Farben built a synthetic rubber and oil plant complex called Monowitz close to the Auschwitz concentration camp. Inmates worked as slave laborers for IG Farben. When they were too weak to work they were killed in the gas chambers. IG Farben subsidiary Degesch manufactured Zyklon B, the gas used in the concentration camp gas chambers.

Bayer head Carl Duisberg personally propagated forced labor during WW1I The company placed itself under a large burden of guilt due to its heavy involvement in the planning, preparation and implementation of both world wars. The International War Crimes Tribunal pronounced the company guilty for its share of responsibility in the war and the crimes of the Nazi dictatorship.

On 29 July 1948, sentences for mass murder and slavery were handed down at the Nuremberg trials to twelve Farben executives. The longest sentence of only seven years was dealt out was to Dr. Fritz ter Meer, a top executive and scientist on the IG Farben managing board After the war, IG Farben separated into three giant corporations: Bayer, Hoechst and BASF. On 1 August 1963, Bayer celebrated its 100th anniversary at the Cologne fairgrounds. The opening speech was mass murderer relevant to the position of Chairman of the Supervisory Board of Bayer. More than eight million people had to do slave work for the Nazi war industry, and none ever received compensation from the companies or the government. David Fishel, one of the few survivors of the camp, sued the companies for compensation. When he was 13 he was forced to work for IG Farben carrying 50-kilo bags of coal and cement when he weighed only 75 pounds.

IG Farben also conducted experiments on humans. Eva Mozes Kor, among the 1,500 sets of twins experimented on by the infamous Dr. Josef Mengele, claims that IG Farben monitored and supervised medical experiments at the Nazi concentration camp where she was interned. She claims the experiments involved toxic chemicals that IG Farben (Bayer) provided. In some of the experiments, the lawsuit states, prisoners were injected with germs known to cause diseases, 'to test the effectiveness of various drugs' manufactured by IG Farben. Mengele conducted genetic experiments there in an effort to create a super race of blonde, blue-eyed Aryans who would be born as a triplet.

Both Kor and her sister survived their 10-month ordeal in the concentration camp and were liberated by Soviet troops in January 1945. They were nearly 10 years old. According to Irwin Levin (Kor's Lawyer), IG Farben paid Nazi officials during World War II for access to those confined in the camps and collaborated in Nazi experiments as a form of research and development.

The lawsuit sought unspecified punitive damages and the recovery of profits it maintains IG Farben (Bayer) earned as a result of such research.

Eventually Eva Kor and various others were paid out of a fund put up by the German government and the companies. Bayer gave 100 million German Marks to the fund. The entire fund (totaling 10 billion German Marks) was a result of various American lawsuits – without the loss of reputation in the US the companies would never have agreed.

a

BAYER IN A NUCLEAR AGE

December 6, 1941 (the day before the Pearl Harbor attack) President Roosevelt signed an order to pursue the development of an atomic bomb. This decision was made, in large part, because of the impending threat of the development of a German nuclear industry. The possible development of a Japanese atomic bomb presented another danger. Although Germany never exploded an atomic bomb the threat of an atom bomb was real. IG Farben was a major part of that effort.   In the post war trials executives of Bayer were among those convicted.

This bomb did not simply end a war it ignited a new form of war which continues to this day. In August 1949 the Soviet Union exploded its first atomic bomb. Four years later (June 1953) Julius and Ethel Rosenberg were executed for allegedly passing secrets to the Soviet Union about the atomic bomb. The atom bomb, supposedly built to end a major war and prevent future wars, was now a tool which could cause even greater war and destruction than had even been imagined.

Not only was war more of a possibility, the bomb had created a major tension between the United States and the Soviet Union. "The bomb" had also ignited not simply a fear and mistrust of the Soviet Union, there was also a growing mistrust of ordinary citizens toward each other. Senator Joseph McCarthy began a series of hearings aimed at exposing and persecuting Communist spies within our Government and the general public. The House Un-American Activities Committee conducted several years of investigations of persons and groups they believed to be subversive.

One of the more notorious cases was the trial of Julius and Ethel Rosenberg. They were executed because it was believed their release of information to the Soviet Union is what enabled Russia to create its own atomic bomb. Later evidence has shown that some of the persons who testified against the Rosenbergs had lied. It is also now clear that the information given by Julius Rosenberg was not significant information. Soviet spies had already learned the information Rosenberg released.

Julius Rosenberg was aware of this mania. Commenting on the sentence given to them, Julius Rosenberg claimed the case was a political frame-up. The following quote is attributed to him just prior to his execution:

"This death sentence is not surprising. It had to be. There had to be a Rosenberg case, because there had to be an intensification of the hysteria in America to make the Korean War acceptable to the American people. There had to be hysteria and a fear sent through America in order to get increased war budgets. And there had to be a dagger thrust in the heart of the left to tell them that you are no longer gonna get five years for a Smith Act prosecution or one year for contempt of court, but we're gonna kill ya!" Letter of Julius Rosenbery as quoted in . Retrieved June 15, 2013

Today there are at least 15000 nuclear bombs. More recent figures suggest 16000 - 17000 weapons. The Secretary General of the United Nations sets the figure at 20000. Whatever figure is correct, a lot of good could be done with money used for nuclear weapons. The USA and Russia own almost 90% of these bombs. At least 9 nations now possess bombs. It is believed that other nations and some terrorist groups have essential ingredients for create nuclear bombs.

Who is responsible today for the continuation of nuclear weapons? Certainly Bayer has to take some responsibility. It provided material used in World War II. It continues to provide material which kills people and keep the cold war going. There are also investors who support the war industry. Between 2011 and 2014 the largest investors invested over 400 billion dollars in war related ventures. Many investors were banks. Investors would not exist if there were nothing in which they could invest. Military related corporations fill that need. IS USA HEADED TOWARD THIS NEW WORLD ORDER? If a serious financial status n indicates the nation is moving toward a "new world order" the USA is certainly moving in that direction. The chart below shows that.

PRESIDENT	STARTING DEBT	CLOSING DEBT	INCREASE
Eisenhower	**$269 billion**	$289.9 billion	$20;9 billion
Kennedy	$289.9 billion	$305.8 billion	$15.9 billion
Johnson	$308.8 billion	$434.7 billion	$128.9 billion
Nixon/Ford	$434,7 billion	$698.8 billion	$264.1 billion
Carter	$698.8 billion	. $997.8 billion	$299.0 billion
Reagan	$997.8 billion	**$286** trillion	$1.86 trillion
Bush 1	**$2.86** trillion	$4.41 trillion	**$1.55** trillion
Clinton	$4.41 trillion	$65.67 trillion	$1.26 trillion
Bush 2	$5.67 trillion	$15.02 trillion	$9.35 trillion
Obamat	$15.52 trillion		

There are other indication of a struggling (if not dying) U.S. economy. Several reports that 35% of Americans are on welfare Depending on how the reporting group measures "welfare" the percentage ranges from 9% 35% Those for a lower measurement do not say there is not a problem. The following chart shows an economic pattern in the assassination of US presidents.

Jackson	Madman no reason	shut down central bank
Lincoln	John Wilkes Booth Civil War	Green Backs replace current currency
Kennedy	Lee H. Oswald: Cuban policy	K restore to President control of money

This chart shows an economic reason for every attempt to eliminate a U.S. President. Jackson escaped the attempt.to kill him. For every was we can find an economic reason for the war. This reason is usually not apparent until the war ends. Settlement of the two major world wars led to the creation of international world bank: World War 1 -Bank for International Settlements World War 2 - the World Bank.

There was (late August 2015) a debate in the U.S. Congress whether to continue funding the Export Import Bank charter. That bank has never been threatened with a shutdown. It has been shut down for two months already. In late summer the U.S. stock market fell nearly 1000 points. The stock market in China has experienced a similar fall.

The U.S. Congress has been forced to reset is budget every 6 month and set a limit on how much the budget may be increased. Every one of these warning items could be averted. When all come together in a short time it is hard to deny that we need to make some drastic changes. The economic reason is often disguised under a more politically acceptable reason as the following chart shows about recent US wars.

Nation	Reason given for US in war	REAL reason
Syria	Has bomb Hussein a tyrant	Moved oil backed currency to Euros
Lybia	Gaddaffi	He moved money to own central bank
Iraq	Has nuclear bomb is unsafe	Iran threat to US economic superiority
Oil rich nations	Varies	US wants oil to back weak currency instead of gold

The US Government is quick to attempt to justify aggressive attitude to foreign nations without telling us the REAL reason our leaders involve us in foreign wars, the economic reasons. The above chart help unveil some of the unanswered questions.

Korean "Conflict"

At the time it was being fought there was an attempt to pretend it was not really a war, just a conflict! Whatever we choose to call it, there were thousands of human persons killed. Thousands of persons were exiled and others made profits from the conflict/war.

How did this "conflict" begin? For several years before the Second World War ended all of Korea was a single nation controlled by Japan. As the European part of the war ended the USA and Russia were allies. Both nations were united in a common cause – the defeat of Hitler and Nazism.

After the German surrender Japan still needed to be subdued. There was little doubt they would be beaten. Three months after Germany surrendered two atomic bombs were dropped on Japan. Within a few days Japan surrendered. This surrender meant (among other things) who now controlled Japan?

Before the Second World War ended three major conferences were held. Although other nations were involved, attention was focused on the head to the two nations best equipped to deal with cleanup of the damage left from World War Two (USA and Russia). The most pressing question was what to do with Korea, still a single nation. Should it be under the control of the USA or the control of Russia?

A U.S. military official arbitrarily defined the division at the 36th parallel. Land north of the 38th parallel was controlled by Russia. Land south of the 38th parallel was controlled by the USA. Initially both Russia and the USA were agreeable to this division. The people of Korea were never consulted on this decision.

Within a short time problems created by this "solution" began to emerge. What was once a single nation was now North Korea and South Korea. Families were split: family members north of the arbitrary line were separated from members to the south. What was once a "solution" between two super powers became an international war. Russia was unable to maintain Korea and involved an ally, China. The USA persuaded the United Nations to support them. The war became an international ideological contest between socialism and capitalism.

The differences between the groups occupying Korea became so intense that people were not permitted to pass from one side to the other.

Editor's note: This same ideological difference has continued to be used to justify an ongoing financial conflict – not just in Korea!

After years of conflict and its ensuing loss of life, destruction of land, separation of families the "settlement" of the war was a division of the two nations at the 38th parallel. (SURPRISE!!!) The war ended but its implications continue to this day. If we follow the 38th parallel west from Korea we will find countries with rich natural resources also divided by this arbitrary decision at the end of World War two.

We find many of these nations have nuclear bombs. A large number of these nations divide Islamic groups from Christian groups. This is one of the prime sources of war. All of these divisions are a consequence of the 38th parallel agreement. That agreement was more an economic agreement than a political or ideological one. Then we wonder why terrorist groups bombed Wall Street rather than the seat of government.

Another consequence of the 38th parallel agreement is North Korea. We have not heard much about North Korea until it was announced that they launched a nuclear bomb. Even more formable is cyberwarfare which evolved with the development of more sophisticated computer technology. Even though a poorer and less developed nation, North Korea became one of the leaders in the use of cyberwarfare.

Cyberwarfare

Apart from a few movies cyberwarfare is not a commonly discussed subject. But if it widely used, it could make traditional military warfare obsolete. What is cyberwarfare?

According to Wikipedia: "Cyberwarfare has been defined as "actions by a nation-state to penetrate another nation's computers or networks for the purposes of causing damage or disruption," but other definitions also include non-state actors, such as terrorist groups, companies, political groups" op.cit. According to one report North Korea is the third largest user of cyberwarfare.

Time magazine says "America has spent decades and trillions of dollars building up the greatest military force the world has ever seen. But the biggest threat to national security these days comes not from aircraft carriers or infantry divisions, but a computer with a simple internet connection. That became much clearer after the catastrophic hack—most likely by a foreign power—of sensitive federal employee data stored online."

The article also states "... the U.S. Director of National Intelligence ranks cyber crime as the No. 1 national security threat, ahead of terrorism, espionage and weapons of mass destruction." emphasis added. The above quotes appear in a Time website:
http://time.com/3928086/these-5-facts-explain-the-threat-of-cyber-warfare/

One of the major issues listed on the internet at present (April 2016) is the conflict between North Korea and Sony re: release of a move "the interview". I viewed several accounts of the conflict. None of them discussed how any aspect of cyberwarfare is involved, what are the threats to the USA or North Korea as a result of the movie being shown? This is a usual case of one side blaming the other for the problem. There seems to be little sense of how cyberwarfare is carried on. Many, if not all, of the U.S. Government Departments have whole staffs devoted to preventing cyberwarfare.

There are many more problems posed by cyberwarfare than who controls the release of a movie. For example, could a nation or other group use cyberwarfare against members of its own people?
Didn't we have cyberwarfare even before the process was available? Weren't the "McCarthy Hearings" a form of cyberwarfare? Wasn't hiding or distorting information about alternative energy a form of cyberwarfare? Isn't justifying war by creating false enemies an act of cyberwarfare?

Our entire monetary system is based on money that really isn't there (and simply used to create more false money for the banks and other institutions). Isn't this the ultimate form of cyberwarfare, at least a very major factor in its creation and use by nations and other groups? A new HP [Hewlett Packard] report suggests the reclusive country' warfare capabilities are rapidly making North Korea a credible threat to Western systems.

As cyberattacks will therefore be attributed to the country's governing body, HP says that many attacks sponsored by the regime originate from other countries, including China, the US, Europe and even South Korea. (emphasis added) Material from <u>North Korea Cyber Warfare Capabilities Exposed</u> by Charles Osborne for <u>Zero Day</u> Sept 2. 2014

According to Wikipedia: "A zero-day (also known as zero-hour or 0-day) vulnerability is a previously undisclosed <u>computer-software vulnerability</u> that hackers can adversely affect computer programs, data, additional computers or a network. It is known as a "zero-day" because once the flaw becomes known, the software's author has zero days in which to plan and advise any mitigation against its exploitation.

Attacks employing zero-day <u>exploits</u> are often attempted before or on the day that a notice of the <u>vulnerability</u> is released to the public; sometimes before the author is aware or has developed and made available corrected code. Zero-day attacks are a severe threat. op. cit. Author's note: Is "Zero Day" which published quoted the above this text the name of a magazine or is it a publication of a "Zero Day" organization? There are many more problems posed by cyberwarfare than who controls the release of a movie. For example, could a nation or other group use cyberwarfare against members of its own people? Our entire monetary system is based on money that really isn't there (and is simply used to create more false money for the banks and other institutions). Isn't this the ultimate form of cyberwarfare, at least a very major factor in its creation and use by nations and other groups?

Cyberwarfare is basically distorting, destroying or hiding information in order to direct an individual or a group to act in a way they do not want to act. We do not need highly sophisticated computer systems to do that. (cf. a few examples in the previous paragraph). Modern sophisticated systems make it easier. They allow the user to be more anonymous.

Like many other inventions and systems it is neither good nor bad. The determining factor is how it is used. Several authors list energy, finance, telecommunications, transportation, and water as the foremost tools for cyberwarfare. The U.S. Government has used energy and finance against our own people. One of the tools it has used is telecommunications.

The problems created by cyberwarfare would be less problematic if its use were confined to government action. There is now an international bank (the Bank for International Settlements) that controls the amount of money in circulation and where that money goes. In addition to a huge international bank, there are persons who create or distort the system that runs a bank without human or supervision.

A talented dealer of cyberwarfare could direct that money to sources other than ones for which it was intended. In our own nation the Federal Reserve Bank can (as the Bank for International Settlements) direct funding to nations and groups which enhance their activity. Both banks are totally immune from any outside supervision. The possibility for the use of either bank is limitless. While emphasis on the use or misuse of cyberwarfare is focused on any government using or misusing a form of cyberwarfare little attention is paid to the institutions which fund the abuse. Despite the dangers posed by cyberwarfare, not much attention seems to be paid to the use of cyberwarfare by banks.

The abuse by banks may not be recognized as cyberwarfare but they use the same tools as other abusers of cyber. A significant amount of the money banks transferred can be utilized for war.

Several internet sites speak of the monetary/cyberwarfare connection e.g. <u>Wall Street Oblivious to Cyber-Economic Warfare</u>

An American Council for Democracy report: <u>Cybersecurity and Economic, Financial, and Market Warfare</u> at their ACD/EWI briefing on Cyber Threats and the Economy (April 9, 2013) states: "... financial markets are one of the battlefields on which future wars will be fought."

"Financial war is a form of non-military warfare which as terribly divisive as a bloody war but in which no blood is actually shed."

The Vernalabilities of Developed States to Economic Cyber Warfare
a working paper
by Dr. Paul Cornish
Professor of International Security
Chatom House
Composed March 2008 delivered June 2011

For all the death and destruction they cause these activities could nevertheless all be described as <u>tactical</u> or <u>operable</u> variants of economic warfare

To the extent that the opponent might be dependent on aspects of a functioning economy for access to food, water, transportation, ammunition, and military equipment it can make sense militarily ... to attack and destroy the economic infrastructure which produces these commodities or provides the service for the deliverance to economic cyber warfare."   End of Quote

It does not take too much browsing on the internet to discover how widely cyberwarfare is used, how indetectible is the harm done by cyber ware or the origin of it. Banks have developed their own cyber network by which they can spy on other banks, store investors in a "deep pool" and minipulate the price of the stoke without any of its employees knowing what happened. There was a story in the news about a young boy playing with his computer was able to discern very secretive material from the U.S. military. If it is that easy how can any us be safe?

For more information see <u>Flash Boys A Wall Street Revolt</u> by Michael Lewis

This book began with a look at the role war has played in our history, who profited from war and other aspects of war. This section has described a modern war which it would be virtually impossible to describe. There are no documents. We cannot even list the players. The final part of the book is entitled "Is There any Hope" It describes courageous persons and groups try to create alternatives to this mind blowing scenario we have inherited.

IS THERE ANY HOPE?

We may not be able to change the world in which we live but there are individuals and groups who make a sizeable contribution to its change. Ghandi was a man who made an immense contribution to making the world a little better. He defined seven capital sins that are sins which kill a society. Each of those capital sins is not something we do wrong, but describes something good we do NOT do. We can help by doing the "withouts" of Ghandi's capital sins. They are

politics without principle
wealth without work
commerce without morality
 pleasure education without character
 science without humanity
 worship without sacrifice

Each of the "withouts" is something we can all do. They are qualities which will teach our young people in a far more profound way than all the evils mentioned above. Until a significant number of us provide Ghandi's "withouts" there will be no change There are individual and groups who are practicing the necessary virtues and making profound changes.

GANDHI In his lifetime he was able to make profound changes in the social structure of India. Many of these changes have taken place after his death. Gandhi was not an elected person but he was a man of principle. Was not a man of wealth. His wealth was in the good he was able to do for others. He was not a man of commerce but he was a moral man. His morality was not based on keeping laws but on the law of love for all persons - even of that law violated civil law.

Pleasure without conscience does not mean we should never have pleasure. It means that our pleasure should always come in the form of being moral and finding our please in working for the benefit of others. That was one of Gandhi's qualities. Gandhi was educated in the usual sense. He was educated as a lawyer, however he had character and used his education for the benefit of all the people.

He used his knowledge of science to help all of humanity, to help free them from oppression. His worship was not manifest in going to church. He was willing to make what sacrifice in order to help others understand that there is a being who calls usto respect the life we have all received. These qualities are something every person can imitate.

Yeonmi Park

Yeonmi Park is an inspiring and challenging person for everyone in the world. At age 22 she has spoken in several nations throughout the world. She has come to be known as the "Advocate for North Korea". She is truly that. She could also be the "Advocate for Humanity". Her story calls every person to overcome fear, guilt, shame, and doubt so we do not allow our weaknesses and differences to define who we are.

Yeonmi was born in North Korea 22 years ago. She had no knowledge of the environment in which was born. She knew nothing of the "cold war", nothing of her nation's history or the struggles her nation had experienced. Korea had been a single united nation. More than 50 years before she was born, Korea was divided. There was a war for control of Korea. (Korean War) The "truce" at the end of World War 2 divided Korea at the 38th Parallel.

This "truce" did not settle the conflict between the main forces. The USA favored South Korea. The USSR favored North Korea. She knew nothing of this ideology and political split. She knew nothing about the vast numbers of nuclear weapons that could destroy the world. She could neither read nor write. Her world was limited by her neighborhood. By the standard of most of the world she and her family were poor. Her father dad acquired some money. By local standards she was not poor.

Then, her father was imprisoned because he angered government officials. He and his family we stripped of all money. Her mother was arrested because of her relationship to her husband. When her mother was released she went to find Yeonmi's father. So, in the midst of winter she and her sister lived in a house which had no heat and no food. They were only able to survive because her neighbor (as poor as Yeonmi and her sister) fed them. Because if the environment in which they were forced to live Yeonmi decided to flee to China and begged Yeonmi to go with her. Yeonmi refused to go. When their mother returned she had been unable to find her husband and her daughter had fled. She decided to take Yeonmi and go to China and find her daughter who had fled. It was a difficult decision. The border to China was closed and armed soldiers guarded the border of the river which separated the two nations. She told of a person who would assist them in their escape.

When they made it to China they immediately were met by someone who separated then and sold each of them to men who wanted them as prostitutes. Yeonmi was six years old at the time. The man to whom Yeonmi was sold attempted to rape her. She continued to resist him.

Eventually he managed to rape her. He was so impressed with her courage he decided to free her and help her find her mother. He freed her and helped Yeonmi and her mother to flee from China.

Their escape from China did not end the story. They were forced to go through other countries to flee to South Korea. They were in constant fear of being found and returned to North Korea. Once they reached South Korea they were detained and subjected to intense questioning. Some many persons had fled from North Korea that South Korean border guards were very careful whom they allowed to enter South Korea.

Eventually both were allowed to enter. Yeonmi could not read or write, so she could not enter even the lowest level of school. Her mother was unable to find work. Yeonmi began to study on her own. She was able to qualify for the lowest level of school. Due to her determination she quickly qualified for the highest level. A TV person was doing a series of programs about persons who had fled from North Korea. He invited Yeonmi to appear on the program. He was so impressed with her story that he invited her to do a series of programs. Yeonmi was reluctant. She decided to do it because this might help find her sister.

Her story reached other nations with the help of international television. She was invited to different nations. She became known as the "ADVOCATE for North Korea." Her aim was always to free the people of North Korea. Yeonmi came to the United States and set up an internet site www.yeonmi.net. and a blog www.facebook.com/OfficialYeonmiPark Despite her fame Yeonmi's story does not end here. Her real story will be good she is able to do. Like all of us she had personal obstacles to overcome. She had never consented to the rape. Still, she felt guilty for the rape. Many times she had told her story but she had always omitted the account of the rape. One time as she was about to speak she tore up her notes and told her whole story, even the rape. Only then did she feel free. A book tells the whole story of Yeonmi.

In Order To Live: A North Korean Girl's Journey to Freedom

The book can be found at most major book stores. Her story will only be completed when many other persons are inspired to over their own struggles and the struggles created by their oppressors.

Hiroshima Project

In 1945 Hiroshima, Japan was devastated by a blast of an atomic bomb. Citizens of Hiroshima are acutely aware of the effect of that bombing. They are also aware that it could happen again. They have established a peace museum to promote world peace. They have also established a program "Mayors for Peace". Over 5000 mayors across the world have joined this movement. One of the websites of the Hiroshima effort says this:

The abolition of nuclear weapons cannot be left to nations alone. International public opinion must be formed to lead national policies toward disarmament. Individuals must be committed to peace and determined to build a society free from nuclear weapons. People engaged in a wide variety of related activities must strengthen their solidarity and work together with others around the world. The efficacy of such cooperation was amply demonstrated by the vital role played by non-governmental organizations (NGOs) in establishing the International Treaty Banning Anti-personnel Landmines and in promoting the World Court Project. The latter led to the advisory opinion from the International Court of Justice that says "...the threat or use of nuclear weapons would generally be contrary to the rules of international law." Only the collective power of an inspired populace can move nations, move the United Nations, and lead to a peaceful world. (from Hiroshima/Nagasaki peace site)

In January, 2008 I was contacted by the group and hosted three persons from Hiroshima, Japan for four days. One guest was a victim of the atomic bombing in Hiroshima in 1945. In 2008 she and other victims of the bombing went throughout the United States speaking of their experience, the after effects of the bombing, and present dangers the human race faces from nuclear expansion. Their message has been heightened by recent earthquakes in Japan and the consequent problems not from nuclear bombs but simply from nuclear energy.

Several years later I was asked to give a presentation on my book Why We Are Always Broke. I began by saying: "... for the whole creation is waiting with eagerness ... with the intention that the whole creation itself might be freed from its slavery to corruption and brought into the same glorious freedom as the children of God", (Romans 8:21).

The atomic bombs dropped on Japan left a severe scar on the face of the earth. Before the Atomic bomb was dropped Hiroshima and Nagasaki were ordinary towns. Residents had no idea of what was about to happen. People got up that morning went to work. The children went to school. The bombs dropped on Japan in August 1945 were called atomic bombs. This is because its energy came from the release of atoms that collide with a substance called uranium. This collision results in the release of large amounts of energy in the form of heat.

On the morning of Aug. 6, 1945 the bomb was dropped on Hiroshima, three days later Nagasaki was bombed. The cloud that formed from the bombing looked innocuous enough, and apart from its size and almost perfect mushroom shape it does not look much different from smoke released from any other source of heat.

What the cloud doesn't show is the ball of heat contained within a ball of heat that burns human bodies, buildings, and everything in its way. What had a few minutes earlier been a thriving city was now a bundle of ruins. About 40 percent of the population was killed instantly and many more died of radiation and cancer over the years.

All children, not just children in the womb, were affected by the bomb. Sadako Susaki was 2 years old when the bomb hit. She survived! In 1949 she entered school. Sadako was strong. She could outrun the other children. At age 12 Sadako was diagnosed with leukemia. She believed that she could overcome this sickness. She made a pledge to make 1,000 paper cranes for her survival. She was only able to make 750. Her story became known worldwide. Children from all over the world helped her make the missing paper cranes. From this project an international Children's Peace Museum was born.

The effect of these bombs left a severe scar on the face of the earth – not simply upon Japan – but also, where the first atomic explosion was released in a New Mexico desert. J. Robert Oppenheimer, head of the project was reported to have said, "I have become Death, Destroyer of Worlds." ARE WE JUST HELPLESS VICTIMS? WHAT CAN WE DO? The Hiroshima group also offers a "Peace Studies" program to incorporate into classes in colleges and universities.

International Occupy Movement

As the Occupy Movement was getting organized I spent one night camping out with the Occupy group in Nashville Tennessee. As we finished breakfast I noticed five men in business suits taking pictures of the group. I was curious and went over to talk to them. They were from Germany and come by to take pictures to show to a German Occupy group. One of the men told me; "This is very necessary." This was my first indication that Occupy was a worldwide movement.

I was able to discover some information about the movement in other nations. In England, an Occupy activist won a seat for the City of London Corporation, also known as "The Square Mile Authority." This is the body that governs London's equivalent of Wall Street. The Archbishop of Canterbury spoke strongly in support of that effort and the work of Occupy. Another group protested the huge cost of the Olympic Games while people are starving.

In Madrid, Spain the group was able to force a criminal investigation of Rorigo Rato, CEO of Spain's fourth largest bank. He is also former head of the International Monetary Fund.

In Athens, Greece a group of workers are attempting to take over and claim ownership of a plant that has been closed for nearly a year. In Cairo, Egypt a candidate who supports the ideas proposed by Occupy was elected president. Even in Russia the idea seems to be taking roots as people are occupying public spaces to protest declining economic conditions. There are also local groups still working for economic equality.

Micah White was a co-founder of Occupy Wall Street He describes how devastated he was when the movement was shut down. He is quoted as saying that after the Movement was shut down the mainstream spread around the world It seemed the revolution was at hand. But while some protesters held on for several months, pushing their message of economic inequality, Occupy fizzled, and the status quo remained In late 2011, when police moved in to evict Occupy protesters and their tents from financial districts and public parks around the world, Micah White was devastated.

White had co-founded the original protest in New York City while working for Adbusters magazine, and as a lifelong activist he had dreamt of a new, defiant action that would spark a movement and go IRL viral. So when Occupy Wall Street hit the mainstream, picking up where the Arab Spring had left off, and spread around the world, it seemed the revolution was at hand. But while some protesters held on for several months, pushing their message of economic inequality, Occupy fizzled, and the status quo remained.

But White continued, he wrote a book "The End of Protest" in the book he calls for a new approach *"Protest is broken. Recent years have witnessed the largest protests in human history. Yet these mass mobilizations no longer change society. Now activism is at a crossroads: innovation or irrelevance."*
Cf. Penguin Random House
 https://www.penguinrandomhouse.com/authors/276053/micah-white

In an interview Michael White was asked why he is calling for an end to protests. He states: "The simple answer is basically that these forms of protest that we are kind of ritually repeating are broken. They don't work. And we know that because when we've taken them to the furthest possible conclusion like we did with the Occupy Wall Street, creating a social movement that spread to 82 countries, it didn't create the social change that we wanted. So, I'm calling for the end of protest as we know it because that's the only way to revive the possibility of social change and create new forms of protest, new forms of activism."

He was asked if examples of successful protest didn't disprove this

"We changed the discourse. We raised awareness. We did these things. But those are things that I would associate with social marketing, the idea of getting ideas out there, and not the revolutionary goals of activism which is to, you know, change the regime in power, to put the people in power."

In an interview Michael White was asked why he is calling for an end to protests. He states: "The simple answer is basically that these forms of protest that we are kind of ritually repeating are broken. They don't work.

And we know that because when we've taken them to the furthest possible conclusion like we did with the Occupy Wall Street, creating a social movement that spread to 82 countries, it didn't create the social change that we wanted. So, I'm calling for the end of protest as we know it because that's the only way to revive the possibility of social change and create new forms of protest, new forms of activism."

He was asked if examples of successful protests didn't disprove this "We changed the discourse. We raised awareness. We did these things. But those are things that I would associate with social marketing, the idea of getting ideas out there, and not the revolutionary goals of activism which is to, you know, change the regime in power, to put the people in power."

So, it's not enough to make people aware 1% controls 99%

"If you make noise, you know, if you drop a pebble in the ocean, it still makes ripples. But we shouldn't mistake those ripples for a tsunami. We shouldn't start thinking that just because people are talking about something that somehow it's created some sort of revolutionary change ... And I think there's been a trick that was played on Occupy, which was basically to tell Occupiers, "Hey, you guys didn't fail, you raised awareness," but that's the kind of game that the progressive left and the reformist left plays to keep you from realizing that, oh, actually we failed to achieve the revolutionary goal. And I think that's because the progressive left doesn't actually believe in revolution anymore. They don't believe it's possible, they don't think it's desirable and they're more content to play a kind of loyal oppositional role."

cf. Micah M. White @ http//."www.micahmwhite.com

EDITOR'S PERSONAL NOTE

After 12 years of parish work I was allowed to work in a social justice ministry. I built two solar houses in order to show others that it is possible to be less dependent on utility companies. I began working with a man who was rebuilding houses of low income persons. One house was a house of my neighbor. We cut her electricity bill by 60%. We did several houses and saw that rates had risen so high that they were paying almost as much of their 40% electricity as for 100%.

We shifted our focus to the group which set the rates (the Louisiana Public Service Commission). We began attending their meetings. We presented material no one else was sending. Two of the 5 members asked our group to meet with them once a month. I had more free time that the other members. A large part of my work was to do research we could present to the Commission. I begin research on the various companies who owned or had monetary investments in the industry.

I used information the companies were sending each year to the Federal Government (their proxy statements). One Company was Holiday Inn. In one of their proxy statements they told the federal government they had borrowed a large sum of money. That was a large debt they now were obliged to pay. They then borrow the same amount of money they had borrowed to obtain another loan – borrow money on a debt!
I read the statement several times thinking I had made a mistake. When I realized it was not a mistake it finally struck me. The solution for which I hoped to find alternatives lay in the financial field. No one seemed to be pursuing that goal until the occupy movement began. As it died other local groups began to spring up – groups in New York State, Illinois, Oregon and others. Several larger groups began to emerge. A week-long rally in Washington D.C. drew a large crowd and 400 persons were arrested. An international rally is planned for May 1 2016. Occupy has spurned a movement that is not going to die.

Mayors for Peace

In 2010 the U.S. Conference of Mayors passed a resolution asking President Obama to work with world leaders for the total elimination of ALL nuclear weapons by the year 2020. The Mayors cite international organizations which call for the elimination of all nuclear weapons by 2020. They Mayors' resolution concludes:

"NOW, THEREFORE, BE IT RESOLVED that the U.S. Conference of Mayors call on President Obama to work with the leaders of the other nuclear weapons states to implement the U.N. Secretary
General's Five Point Proposal for Nuclear Disarmament forthwith, so that a Nuclear Weapons Convention, or a related set of mutually reinforcing legal instruments, can be agreed upon and implemented by the year 2020, as urged by Mayors for Peace; and
BE IT FURTHER RESOLVED that the U.S. Conference of Mayors calls on the U.S. Senate to ratify the new START treaty and the Comprehensive Test Ban Treaty without conditions and without delay; and   BE IT FURTHER RESOLVED that the U.S. Conference of Mayors encourages President Obama, members of the Cabinet and Congress to visit Hiroshima and Nagasaki at the earliest possible date.

Again, although it is an international effort it is sustained locally.   Every reader can work with local officials to sustain the movement. Without that local support the movement will die.

North Dakota State Bank

The State of North Dakota set up its own bank, the Bank of North Dakota. The Bank was opened in 1918 because of a populist movement that spread across the State. It was, in large part, a reaction against the money lords especially in the eastern US. These lords decided who got money, as well as how goods would be marketed. As part of that reaction a movement, the Non-partisan -9League, took control of the North Dakota Legislature, They created the Bank of North Dakota as a financing arm. They created a state-owned mill and elevator to market and buy grain from the farmer.

According to its official charter, the "state of North Dakota shall engage in the business of banking, and for that purpose shall maintain a system of banking owned, controlled, and operated by it, under the name of the Bank of North Dakota" The bank is to be governed by the "Industrial Commission" who shall "operate, manage, and control the Bank" "To enlist the help of private enterprise and to encourage more active use of the purposes for which the Bank of North Dakota was created, the governor shall appoint an advisory board of directors to the Bank of North Dakota consisting of seven persons, at least two of whom must be officers of banks, the majority of the stock of which is owned by North Dakota residents, and at least one of whom must be an officer of a state-chartered or federally chartered financial institution.

The charter provides that all State funds must be deposited in this bank. The charter contains the usual precautionary regulations for a business or bank (audits, obligations of directors, treatment of violations etc.). The charter recognizes that the Bank will make a profit. What is unique about this charter is it places a limit (both a monetary limit and a time limit) on loans the Bank may make or indebtedness it may incur. The loan or indebtedness may not be more than ten million dollars and the time may not exceed one year.

Also unique, the Charter defines how the Bank may invest its profits. The profits are to be used for the benefit of the citizens of North Dakota. It specifies loans to new farmers residing in the state, "health care providers to purchase and upgrade electronic health record technology, train personnel in its use, improve security of information exchange, and for other purposes as established by the health information technology office, in collaboration with the health information technology advisory committee."

The Bank may make loans to private home owners. The home must be their primary home. It is for those who otherwise may not be able to obtain such a loan. It may not exceed 200,000 dollars and may not extend more than thirty years. The profits of the bank shall be used to fund educational institutions in the State for those special needs of the one% of the population with specific educational needs. The charter provides for funding persons in the State who are victims of natural disasters in an area declared a disaster zone.

In its history the Bank waxed and waned. Conservative groups constantly fought the bank and tried to destroy is credibility and its effectiveness. More liberal groups would regain control and try to move the Bank forward. In the last few years it became apparent that the banking industry had failed and had led the nation into an economic crisis. Only then did the Bank of North Dakota begin to stand out as a viable alternative. Over the last 10-15 years the Bank has returned over a third of a billion dollars to the State fund for use of the needs of its citizens. That's not bad for a State with 600,000 residents. That would be equivalent to 21 billion dollars in California, over 14 billion dollars in Texas, and 11 billion dollars in New York State.

Forty-eight states currently have budget shortfalls. The common strategy being dictated in many of these states and in Washington is to call for budget cuts, eliminating important safety nets for the middle-class and those below the poverty line, as well as to repeal legislation guaranteeing collective bargain rights for unions. It's as if the states and the federal government were corporations with no responsibility to their real stockholders, the citizens of the U.S. Some States have decided enough is enough; they have introduced legislation for publicly owned banks or derivations, or for studies or task forces to determine how a publicly owned bank would operate in their jurisdiction. Currently several states have introduced legislation to create their own central bank. In every case the banking industry has such a powerful lobby they have been able to defeat the effort. Every reader can help in that effort by putting pressure on local officials to create a state (or county) bank similar to the North Dakota State Bank. The effort will not come from a state legislature. The effort (like the "Mayors for Peace" will grow out of local citizens getting the cities state or counties to create a publicly owned bank. A few years ago I wrote another book. In researching that book I contacted the North Dakota and was told that officials of 47 (of 49) states had contacted the Bank seeking information on how to set up a state owned bank.

Despite bank opposition there is something the ordinary person or group can do. For example: in Illinois a group pushing for publicly owned banks has created their own website www.illinoispublicbanking.orgHYPERLINK

They have this to say of themselves: "We are a group of organizers, activists and citizens who have come together for the purpose of establishing a public bank in Illinois. We are researching the best way and place for this institution. We take our inspiration from the Bank of North Dakota.

As we organize ourselves and expand, this web site will list all our organizers and allies. For now – if you want to participate:

Email Dr. Lora Chamberlain for more information
info@illinoispublicbanking.org
Email Tom Tresser if you want to help or contribute resources
tom@tresser.com

New York State has a website for public banking
http://groups.yahoo.com/group/EconomicReformhttp:

There is also a petition asking people to sign. The petition expresses the sense of common need for some new solutions. It reads in part:

"So, the state is asking to retain $111 billion of public assets instead of paying "New York's $9 billion budget gap" (this figure according to the Times). It's important to understand that any state has literally thousands of various government CAFRs with investments like this. What's required is comprehensive and independent accounting and independent cost-benefit analysis of how much money the public has handed over to all levels of government and how to maximize public benefit.

We didn't elect these people to take our money and "invest" it for us. Government is not a for-profit corporation. It is a massive lie of omission to not reconsider these funds for other uses, including a state-owned public bank, based on the highly successful model in North Dakota, which has had a State Bank since 1919 and is currently the only state in the union to be running a budget surplus.

The primary attack is that pension funds are for pensions and illegal to touch. But, keep in mind that this money is already being invested, and sometimes lost, in risky markets by the advisers New York currently pays nearly $100 million to manage their funds. None of this money is invested specifically in community based New York businesses or needs.

In North Dakota, by contrast, ALL state revenues are invested into State needs: agriculture, housing, student loans etc. Many are significantly less risky than the ventures Wall Street money managers currently "invest" in.

Solution: Set up a New York State Bank, use it to make responsible loans, enable the fractional reserve system to create credit (rather than having private banks create it for us and charge us interest) that will create even more money, and pay off New York's obligations with the profits. Why should we pay $99 million to unconnected parties whose main interest is collecting fees, not benefiting New York? Pennsylvania has no legislation introduced as yet. However, some citizens have created a website:

http://papublicbankproject.org/http://papublicbankproject.org/

That website states: "Our goal is creation of partnership banks (often referred to as "public" banks) in the Commonwealth of Pennsylvania, at the state, county or municipal level, to take back control of our money and public credit, and use it to power widespread locally directed investment in economic development, jobs creation and sources of non-tax revenue to support vital public services."

The State of Washington has introduced a bill to create a state owned bank in the State of Washington. 40 representatives sponsored the bill. It is presently dormant despite forty sponsors. Washington has one of the best websites on state owned banking. The site claims:

"Clearly, our current financial systems, nationwide and in Washington State, aren't working. The gap between the rich and poor is growing; worker lay-offs and state deficits are increasing, and many, people need jobs. The answer to our money problems lies in generating credit. Without credit, economies cannot grow.

Our current banking system is directly connected to big banks. On August 3, 2010, Washington State had 67.8% of its current deposits of 35.4 billion dollars in nine private banks that are headquartered outside the Northwest. Most of our tax money is deposited in the Bank of America. These private banks are in business to make profits for their owners and their shareholders. It is not their mission to supply credit to Washingtonians to start businesses, go to school or buy equipment for their farms. These 9 banks directly benefit from holding Washington's state revenue on their balance sheets. They are able to leverage that money (multiply it many times) to create new loans, including out of state loans and to invest that money on Wall Street.

Although 17 States have introduced legislation to study and/or to institute a State owned public bank in their State, no State has yet passed a bill to that effect. Hawaii, Oregon, Vermont, and Washington State have come closest. 20 other States have at least one citizen who is attempting to co-ordinate efforts in that State to start a publicly owned State bank.

For an overview of the work on establishing public banks in the USA search the website   http://publicbankinginstitute.org/

Jerome Daly vs Montgomery National Bank

On June 8, 1964 Jerome Daly took out a mortgage with Montgomery National Bank in Minnesota. After paying some money on the note, he missed a few payments. By April 21, 1967 he was $467.38 behind on his payment. The bank seized his home and lot. On December 7, 1968 a jury ruled he owed no money because the bank by their own admission had put up no real money. The bank appealed the case and requested copies of the proceedings. The court assessed a $2 fee for the papers. The bank submitted 2 $1 Federal Reserve Notes as a fee for the papers. The Judge (a local Justice of the Peace) and the attorney (Mr. Daly himself) insisted this was not real money and demanded silver or gold coins worth $2 in payment. This really was the central issue of the case.

For several months legal wrangling took place. Throughout the entire process the bank refused to pay in anything but Federal Reserve notes. The Justice of the Peace and Jerome Daly insisted that was not legitimate money – the original decision of the jury. Several court orders ruled that Daly and Justice of the Peace Mahoney were to release the papers. Their refusal led to both of them being charged with contempt of court. On August 22, 1969 Mahoney drowned. Some insist he was poisoned. On July 16, 1971 Daly was disbarred as a lawyer.

We will begin an analysis of this case with the ruling of July 16, 1971 disbarring Daly. In a ruling slightly over 8 pages the Supreme Court of Minnesota never rules on the issue raised by Mahoney and Daly (the legitimacy of Federal Reserve money). Daly is cited because he failed to follow a court order prohibiting him for raising this issue. The ruling says he and the Justice of the Peace had no authority. Furthermore, he does not possess the "qualities of character and the professional competence requisite to the practice of law."

The ruling also says "lawyers are granted a monopoly to perform legal services for hire... they, like all monopolies must be subject to strict regulation.". It charges that Daly has "failed to conduct himself in a manner consistent with the ethical principles of the legal profession ... flaunted his disregard for the authority of judges ... he has offered no persuasive evidence or excuse for his conduct.". Moreover he has "demonstrated a perverted misconception of the role and function of an attorney."

Only once in the court's own statement is the Federal Reserve mentioned. Daly is charged with using the hearing process "as a forum for expounding his own views concerning the constitutionality of the Federal Reserve System and the validity of Federal Reserve notes."

Another direct reference to the Federal Reserve in the court order is in the series of questions they submitted to Daly in a previous hearing.

"Q. Now, Mr. Daly, IF an order was issued out of the Supreme Court of the United States determining that the Federal Reserve System was a constitutionally appropriate system would you follow that order?"

"A: Not if they are going to perpetuate a fraud on the people."

"Q: Let's ASSUME that what they do is to declare the Federal Reserve System is a constitutional system." (emphasis added)

"A: Do you want to know if I would follow that order of the Supreme Court of the United States if they said that the banks had authority to manufacture money and credit out of nothing, you would ask me if I would follow that?" "Q: Yes, sir" "A: I would not."

That is an interesting series of questions. In one question the word IF is used. In the other ASSUME is used. Both mean the condition does not exist at present. So the court has not declared the Federal Reserve constitutional. Daly is not challenged when he asks if the questioner means would I follow an order, even a Supreme Court order that allows the Federal Reserve to manufacture money and create credit out of nothing. That is the essential issue Daly, Mahoney, and the jury raised. No place in the entire disbarment ruling does the court clearly declare the Federal Reserve constitutional. They do not even take this opportunity. They disbar Daly for raising it.

There are two other veiled references to the issue raised by the Jury, Mahoney, and Daly. The order refers to Daly's "fanciful assertions that these proceedings are a conspiracy by banks and their directors to put an end to his persistent attacks upon the constitutionality of the monetary system of the United States." It cites that the purpose is not to "punish an attorney or prevent him from in good faith espousing a legal cause ... but rather to discharge this court's responsibility to protect the public..." It is difficult to envision how the perpetuation of the Federal Reserve "protects the public."

Without mentioning the Federal Reserve the decree charges Daly with using his position to "harass the banks" and "avoid his own legal obligations" These legal obligations refer to income tax. He is cited for failure to list income for 4 years. He is asked if that is correct.

"A. Well, they use the sign dollar, which I understand means dollar. And there were no figures disclosed with reference to income that is right, dollars, as such."

"Q: You interpret the word dollars to mean gold and silver coins received by you?"

"A: Or their equivalent."

"Q: Which would be a certificate redeemable in gold or silver?"

"A: Freely and readily available."

Again, there is no question of someone not understanding what Daly is saying. There is simply an outright rejection of the idea and of Daly's right to espouse the idea.

The above notes are taken from the Minnesota State Law Library http://www.lawlibrary.state.mn.us/CreditRiver/CreditRiver.htmlhttp://www.lawlibr

On December 7, 1968 in a case Montgomery National Bank vs. Jerome Daly, a jury ruled in favor of Jerome Daly. They ruled that the bank (Montgomery National Bank) had no right to seize his house and sell it because they had put up no real money. The jury ruling stated Daly was entitled to recover his land. The mortgage of May 8, 1964 was

declared null and void. The sale of the land by the sheriff was declared null and void. The Bank had no right, title, or interest in the property and a provision of the Minnesota Constitution which limited the authority of this court was repugnant to the constitution of the USA.

http://www.lawlibrary.state.mn.us/CreditRiver/CreditRiver.htmlhttp://www.lawlibrary.state
.mn.us/CreditRiver/CreditRiver.html   )

A memorandum of the Justice of the Peace, Martin Mahoney, brought out the following: the bank president admitted

1. That because of interlocking activities and practices the bank is to be treated as one with the Federal Reserve.

2. Money and credit came into existence only when they created it.

3. No U. S. law gave them the right to do this.

4. Creation of such money was not according to the U. S. Constitution.

Mahoney also maintained:

1. That nothing in the U.S. Constitution limited the authority of the local court.

2. No question of the court's jurisdiction was raised by either party

3. The bank made no complaint that they did not receive a fair trial. .

Since the proceedings of the trial are apparently not in the State's files (at least I could not find them) Mahoney's claims cannot be verified or disproven. Later, material filed by the Bank's lawyer claims he challenged the neutrality of the jurors. Because trial transcripts are unavailable or difficult to find his claims cannot be proved or disproved.

What is most interesting and most pertinent is that, as in the case of the disbarment of Daly, the lawyer's contentions for challenging the decision of the jury does not make any claim that the Federal Reserve notes are real money. The legality of the case is challenged on the following terms:

The State of Minnesota is being sued. The State cannot be sued without its permission.

The State has never given such permission.

Daly has been permanently enjoined from raising this issue.

Daly did not have the right to sue.

The court (a court of the Justice of the Peace) does not have authority over this matter.

Daly paid a portion of the cost of his house so waived all right to sue. Like the Supreme Court judges in their decision, the lawyer (Theodore Mellby) recognizes the basic issue Daly is raising (legitimacy of Federal Reserve notes). He twists this to attempt to prove Daly has no right to sue. Mellby maintains that a person has a right to sue only if (s)he has received a personal direct injury. He contends that Daly is suing not because of a personal direct injury but because of a "quixotic, contention that the Federal Reserve System is unconstitutional". Once again there is no statement that the Federal Reserve System is constitutional, only a statement that non-belief in it is "quixotic".

According to the dictionary the word quixotic does not mean false. It means it is good but is also romantically idealistic, visionary, and impractical.

In over fifty documents available through the Minnesota Law Library it is never stated that the decision of a small court in Minnesota in 1967 is incorrect or false. Much legal maneuvering occurs to discredit the case. But it is never once clearly stated that the Federal Reserve Bank is constitutional. Many opportunities to do so clearly are present. Several accounts that I read suggest that the Justice of the Peace who presided over the case was murdered. It is easy to make a possible connection between his sudden death and the decision he rendered. Such a connection will probably never be proved or disproved.

What makes me suspicious, however, is that four years earlier the President of the United States (John F. Kennedy) not only raised this issue but began to recreate the silver certificate and limit the amount of credit the Federal Reserve could create (Executive Order 11110 June 1963). Within a few months he was murdered. Within a few days the entire process ceased. In the numerous investigations and accounts of his murder I have never seen that listed as a possible cause of his murder.

David Mack

David Mack has an unusual hotline. He advises people and groups how to avoid foreclosures and other economic problems brought on by bank fraud. Below are some of his more pertinent points. When you sign a mortgage, there are players in the game. While you are unaware, there are facts that you are not told.

1) Since the USA declared bankruptcy in 1933, it has no money only debt. All properly in gold was seized by the government as collateral in the bankruptcy of the US.

2) All money is a promise to pay made by the US government.   3) So, the "note" you sign in order to buy a home is placed in your account as money just as it you had placed a $10 Federal Reserve note in your account. So your home is paid for when you sign the note. When you sign a "note" it becomes money.

Mack goes on to describe what happens to your "note" after you sign it. The note does not simply remain in the bank's vault That is when the other players come into the game.

With the loan you are required to sign a "deed of trust" or other "security instrument" which states that you will pay back your loan. The bank then sells this and other mortgages to another buyer and gets paid again - the amount of money that you owe. He raises the question does the bank have the loan agreement and the deed of trust documents signed at the time of the purchase of the house? He claims in most cases no! They have sold them off. All they have are electronic reproductions of the original. He claims the bank, by law, must have original documents in order to foreclose. He mentions that banks have backed off of foreclosure proceedings when the original documents were not there. David Mack refers to 26 foreclosure cases in Ohio which were dismissed because the bank did not have the original records. (emphasis added)

Mack mentions ways the consumer can avoid the process:
1) Demand that the bank produce the original documents. 2) They did not have the original documents. He lists two possible ways to prevent foreclosure party being foreclosed can issue a bonded promissory note. Banks and other representatives of banks claimed these are bogus. I can go on the Internet, type in the state in which I live, and the amount of money I want to create. I am then referred to an attorney who will draft the document. Then I can then deposit it in a bank as money.

David Mack asked why isn't this note legitimate? How is it different from notes that you sign for your home? How is it different from the note that the bank now uses as money to increase its revenues?

Banks have created Mortgage Electronic Regulation System (MERS). Its mother corporation is MERSCORP Holdings, Inc. On Its website it defines itself as a "privately held corporation that owns and manages the MERS® System and all it's other possessions. It is a member-based organization made up of thousands of lender servicers, sub-servicers, investors and government institutions. Mortgage Electronic Registration Systems,

The economic reason is often disguised under a more politically acceptable reason as the following chart shows about recent US wars.

Nation	Reason given for US in war	REAL reason
Syria	Has bomb Hussein a tyrant	Moved oil backed currency to Euros
Lybia	Gaddaffi	Moved money to own central bank
Iraq	Has nuclear bomb is unsafe	Iran threat to US economic superiority
Oil rich nations	Varies	US wants oil to back weak currency instead of gold

Inc. (MERS) serves as the mortgagee in the land records for loans registered on the MERS® System, and is a nominee (or agent) for the owner of the promissory note.

The MERS® System is a national electronic database that tracks changes in mortgage servicing and beneficial ownership interests in residential mortgage loans. "The Board of Directors are exclusively from large financial institutions. These include government financial institutions like Freddie Mac and Fannie Mae. Both of the two financial institutions are owned by the federal government and in danger of indictment.

In an email David Mack sent me the following material he had written:

"Did you know that there is NO money today? If you doubt that think about this. Is there any silver in the coins now like there was up to 1964? NO!! Look at the paper that is in your wallet that you think is money. Read what it says at the top of the "bill" and you will see it says "Federal Reserve Note". What is a note? It is a promise to pay..... it is DEBT! When you use that Note to buy something you are using debt to pay a debt. Does that make sense? Remember when you held "Silver Certificates"? It said right on them they could be redeemed for silver at the US Treasury. Those are no longer in circulation or able to be printed"

Barter groups and co-operatives

An article in <u>Sojurners</u> magazine claims that over 130 million Americans are engaged in co-operatives and/or barter groups. That is almost 40% of the population of the USA. Today there are about 7500 credit unions active in the USA. The have roughly a billion dollars in savings of the members. In the fall of 2011 as the Occupy Movement began there was a push to take money out of huge banks and place the money in credit unions and small local banks.

One of the advantages of the local cooperative or barter group is that it is local. It helps to create community. People begin to help one another, get to know one another, help recognize that they have far more resources available to themselves than they ever realized.

A barter group could be called a "time bank." Instead of depositing money in the bank, people deposit their time. All time is of equal value. It does not matter how society as a whole regards your time. The members recognize that our time is precious whether we cut grass or perform more sophisticated and more highly paid task.

There are barter groups of individual persons. Many towns have local barter groups. As money becomes less available and goods and services become more expensive, more and more barter groups are being formed. Some larger cities (e.g. New Orleans) have barter groups composed of local businesses. Check out your area for a local barter group or groups. I wrote this for an Austin, Texas barter group.

"When I was a youngster with a dollar bill I could get a school lunch, a haircut, a bus ride, and a candy bar. And I still had twenty cents left. Several persons have told me: "We were poor then but we didn't know it. In terms of the amount of money they had, they were poor. In terms of their ability to obtain necessary goods and services they were not poor. That is the truth that "time banks" recognize. One of these "time banks" is the Austin Time Exchange Network (ATEN) in Austin, Texas.

The stated goal of ATEN is "to serve as a bridge between people from different economic, social, and ethnic backgrounds by providing the opportunity for interaction through the exchanging of services. All of this aims to encourage systemic social change, economic equality, and community empowerment in Austin."

The goal of ATEN is not to increase the money supply. It is to serve as a BRIDGE between people from different economic, social and ethnic backgrounds. The reason for building the bridge is not simply exchanging services. The Network is founded to help bring about social change in order to help create economic equality. The basic unit of exchange is a not a dollar which is a debt, but an hour of service which is an asset, not a liability. Rather than a dollar which is created by a central bank, the hour of service is created in the local community by the members of the community. The members create their own currency. This greatly empowers the community.

ATEN and other "time banks" are increasingly necessary because of rising costs and lower incomes. In addition to these obvious difficulties people are more aware that they are taking less care of one another. There was a breakdown of families and of neighborhoods. There was less personal contact. Truly they are more than barter networks. They are "time banks". The time we invest in bettering ourselves and our community. THAT is the real wealth of a community.

While local food production and consumption are on the rise, this represents less than 1% of food production in the USA. This figure is given us by the U.S. Department of Agriculture. It is significantly lower than actual figure. That is not due to deceit on the part of USDA. It simply means they are not really into what is happening in agriculture. They are more into agribusiness.

The USDA estimate does not reflect persons who grow a significant, or even a small portion of their own food. It does not reflect the local food that passes through local barter groups or cooperatives.

I checked "farmers' markets" on the internet. There are almost four million hits under that title. Obviously, I did not check all of the possible websites. I did, however, check several pages. All of the early sites were for local markets in many different cities. There were sites for state confederations of local farmer's market groups. There is a much more significant amount than any USDA estimate would suggest.

While the economics of our time are motivating more and more people to seek local food they are significant other issues involved in local food production. These are well spelled in a website www.turningearthllc.comHYPERLINK "http://www.turningearthllc.com/" w These are some of the facts brought out in the website:

40% of the food produced in the USA is wasted. This figure includes all of our food systems beginning at the farm and ending at the family table. Less than 3% of the food wasted is recycled.

As a result, about 1400 calories of energy per day per person are wasted, 25% of annual U.S. consumption of freshwater water is wasted, 300 million barrels of oil were used to produce this wasted food. There are may website available on the internet. I recommend

www.boggycreekfarm.comHYPERLINK "http://www.boggycreekfarm.com/" www.boggycreekfarm.com

At that website is a reference to

Alternative health care

A few years ago there was a "health care" bill that passed the U.S. Congress. It was narrowly dismissed by the U.S. Supreme Court. The original bill was not about health care. One of the most controversial issues in Congress today is who will pay the enormous and continually rising cost of health care? The original bill overturned by the Supreme Court said little about natural healing and healing in general. It was about the payment of health care services. That is another example laws are not about human care and human health but about money.

Naturopathic medicine operates on certain principles which are health oriented. First, it will do no harm to the patient. I know of persons with addiction to cocaine or other serious drugs. They started out taking "legal" drugs. These legal drugs were not strong enough. They kept using stronger and stronger addictive drugs until they were into illegal drugs. The first principle of naturopathic medicine is: do not give someone a drug or anything that can be harmful.

The next principles of naturopathic medicine are related. They are based on the principle that the best healer is Mother Nature. Our bodies were created so that they heal themselves. So, above all, utilize the healing power of nature. For that to work you must treat the whole person, not simply a symptom which also means you treat the CAUSE of the disharmony. That means a doctor has to take some time with a patient. S/he cannot just prescribe medication on the basis of the symptom the patient shows.

There are three other principles of naturopathic medicine. The first is the doctor and patient must understand that wellness is more than the absence of disease. The next is we need to emphasize prevention.

For example, if you live or work in a very unhealthy environment no amount of drugs or other medical solutions will cure the problem. To succeed in this endeavor the doctor must educate the patient. First all, make the patient understand that s)he is the major healer in his/her own health process.

The patient also needs to become aware that health is a process not a medical solution. Sometimes an illness is spiritual than physical. Until that spiritual illness is dealt with no amount of medication will heal the patient. Another problem with current medicine is that a large percentage of doctors are specialits. They do not treat the whole person. Some with an ailment may have to see 3 or 4, maybe even more for a single illness.

There are also things each of us can do. The following are principles by which naturopathic medicine is practiced:

•Utilize the healing power of nature

•Treat the whole person, not just the disharmony

.Treat .the .cause of the disharmony
•Educate the patient

•Emphasize prevention

•Understand that wellness is more than the absence of disease.

Persons practicing alternative medicine exist throughout the USA, throughout the world. To find out who is doing so in your area go to the internet, type in "alternative medicine" OR "natural healing" AND the name of your city or an area near you. We are not going to become well by spending huge sums of money for exotic cures. We will become well by living in conformity with nature.

Worker owned companies

One group which nicely ties together cooperatives, local food production and worker owned companies is the Ohio Employee Ownership Center. It was started at Kent State University. The project evolved out of a "failure".

In 1977 Youngstown Sheet and Tube was closing its plant in Youngstown, Ohio. A local group was formed to allow the workers to purchase the plant and continue operations. That was a very radical idea in 1977. Leaders realized that they could succeed only if they were to educate large numbers of people about the merits of such a plan. They begin that process of education. One of their leaders said: "Even if we fail, we may put forward an idea that may help other people who might try to do this in other situations." Attempts to convert Youngstown Sheet and Tube into a worker owned company failed, but the failure resulted in the establishment of the Ohio Employee Ownership Center at Kent State University.

The Ohio Employee Ownership Center has mushroomed. Hundreds of companies have been formed and thousands of jobs have been relocated. "This center has helped build an exciting new model for worker ownership: a network in Cleveland of green worker cooperatives, linked to a larger structure that includes metropolitan anchor institutions such as hospitals and universities. This successful project is now dubbed the "Cleveland model." It is catching on all over the country. There are explorations of this in Amarillo, Texas; Atlanta; Pittsburgh; Richmond, California; and Washington, D.C."

Land Trusts

Land trusts have become another popular way of preserving the environment, meeting the needs of local communities, and assuring that the land remains productive for local needs (food, recreation, space etc.). One of the popular websites on land trusts says this: What is a Land Trust?

Land Trusts are local, regional, or statewide nonprofit conservation organizations directly involved in helping protect natural, scenic, recreational, agricultural, historic, or cultural property. Land trusts work to preserve open land that is important to the communities and regions where they operate.

Land trusts respond rapidly to conservation needs and operate in cities, rural, and suburban areas. Land trusts now operate in every state in the nation protecting land of local, regional, and national importance.

Collectively, America's nearly 900 independent land trusts:
• helped protect 2.7 million acres

• own 437,000 acres
• hold conservation easements on another 450,000 acres
• have acquired, protected, and transferred 668,000 acres to other organizations and agencies
• have used other direct methods to help protect another 1,159,000 acres.

Well known areas protected by land trusts include land on the California coast at Big Sur; in the San Juan Islands, Washington State; at Jackson Hole, Wyoming; along the Appalachian Trail; in New York's Adirondacks; and at Acadia National Park in Maine. anting to do either of those. However, that is not the focus of this book. There are even websites to walk you through the process of setting up a land trust. Again, many of them are oriented toward making maximum profit from your land.

The best method for one interested in preserving land would be to go to an index on the internet. Then type in land trust, conservation, and the name of your state. Each state has different guidelines for setting up land trusts.

Business Alliance for Local Living Economies

The Business Alliance for Local Living Economies (BALLE) is North America's fastest growing network of socially responsible businesses, comprised of over 80 community networks in over 30 U.S. states and Canadian provinces representing more than 22,000 locally owned, independent business members. BALLE networks create local living economies through the building blocks of independent retail, sustainable agriculture, renewable energy, green building, local zero-waste manufacturing, and community capital.

AFTERTHOUGHT

At the time of World War Two there was an international banking system – not as wide spread as today – but present.

There was a strong coalition between the Nazis and governments, both established governments and individuals in various governments including the USA.

IG Farben was a substantial financial contributor to Hitler.

Farben reaped huge profits from the war.

Farben was "divided" into 4 different corporations after the war each continued to produce war material

Allen Dulles worked with German and Swiss groups to reshape European banks according to USA interests

OPERATION PAPERCLIP – accounts of Nazi scientists files were changed because they were not to be admitted

Leaders of IG Farben jailed sentences were short, were released earlier "on good behavior"

BASF (I G Farben child) prominent in Nazis made destructive chemical material later made elements to destroy environment; later made elements to clean up their waste

BASF spread throughout world

BAYER used poison gas to kill slaves unable to produce

CYBERWARFARE a way of changing information on computers to place material to opponent – now used by many countries including USA will make wars obsolete

North Korea separated at 38th parallel by USA/USSR agreement became reason for Korean war 38th parallel became dividing line between US and USSR interests that parallel now has numerous nuclear weapons along patallel

The book also contains information about persons and groups trying to create elements to counter wars e.g.

Yaonmi Park 22 year old fled from North Korea at age has spoken in over 30 different nations established website and blog (cf above)

Hiroshima museum international museum to educate persons about Dangers of nuclear weapons aim: to outlaw all nuclear weapons by 2020

Thank you for reading

to obtain copies:

CreateSpace
go to CreateSpace books
type in William Crumley or
Things We Need To Know

Amazon
go to books
type in things we need to know
through Amazon you can reach Kindle

Or you can reach me
bcrumley078@gmail.com
574-631-9568

William Crumley
P.O. Box 1048

Notre Dame, IN 46556-1048

Hope you find the book informative

William Crumley

www.ingramcontent.com/pod-product-compliance
Lightning Source LLC
Chambersburg PA
CBHW081312170526
45166CB00011B/3503